‘Exhale the past, inhale the future’
Magda’s Story

Magdalena Stewart

Published by New Generation Publishing in 2021

First Edition

ISBN

Paperback 978-1-80031-049-0
Ebook 978-1-80031-048-3

www.newgeneration-publishing.com

New Generation Publishing

For my husband – my rock

Contents

1
My 'journey' to my wheelchair

I really am not sure if this will help but it is good to write it down and vent some thoughts that are harassing me.

It all started over four years ago ...

On 10th May 2016 I went to hospital in Edinburgh because I was not able to walk and I was afraid that I would not be able to attend my MRI appointment, which was scheduled for 12th May. We have to go back in time to February 2015 to understand the reason behind me needing an MRI in the first place.

At the beginning of February 2015, I had a brain haemorrhage and was subsequently diagnosed with an AVM (arteriovenous malformation) on my brain stem. Putting it in less official jargon, I had tangled veins on my brain stem where they should not be and they bled. After a while doctors decided what would be the best course of action for such a rare and unknown case like mine (because of the location of my AVM - brain aneurysm). One thing comes to mind: "Lucky me!" At the end of April, I had an operation to resolve the issue with my brain. It was Stereotactic Radiosurgery, a kind of laser beam targeted into my head. It was supposed to be the less risky option, it only took twenty minutes, but it had serious side effects and consequences for my future and my health.

My balance was off and therefore I was not able to walk. Firstly, I was admitted to the oncology department of Western General Hospital (WGH). I was sent to this unit because my neurologist is a radiologist oncologist and the head of this ward too. She was and still is very helpful and worries about me. I spent three weeks there.

I went to another hospital in Edinburgh, straight after my time at WGH. I was ‘lucky’ enough to be ten and a half months in a brain rehab hospital (BRH; my neurologist made sure that there was a space for me), opposed to the two months I had first expected. These were crazy and dark times. The rehab intended to help my brain was hindered by my health constantly declining. I hit rock bottom when I was admitted to WGH with suspicion of psychosis. I have a very vague recollection of these two weeks. They adjusted my medication (a combination of steroids and many painkillers) and I came back to ‘life’. Then I had trouble with breathing and swallowing and therefore eventually I had a feeding tube – a PEG – installed in my stomach. It was bad but necessary, as thanks to it I eventually got my strength back, and finally started my road to recovery.

My stay there (at the BRH) was very emotional, like a rollercoaster ride. At first, I was trying to make sense of what had happened to me. There was one question at the back of my head: "Why me?" I lost so much energy dwelling on my injury and its consequences for me and my life. That is why I had troubles with my rehab, it was not going as fast and efficiently as I had imagined at first, there was always something wrong with me. My health really went downhill. Trips to A&Es of different hospitals became my ‘weekend treats’. I was treated there for high temperature, a blood clot in my left thigh, gluing my left eye which ended up with the partial eye transplant, to name but a few.

I have had lots of different ‘classes’ at the BRH like physiotherapy, physiology and speech therapy among many others. However, they had not brought the expected results, as I mentioned before, my health was declining rapidly. To be perfectly honest, they (in the BRH) did not know what to do with me. At first, I was very sad, frustrated a lot and I was crying constantly because I could not see or imagine my future life. Then, especially during my problems with breathing and swallowing, I simply did not care about all that, I just wanted not to be scared to swallow and choke.

The female only ward became kind of my home for quite long time. I shared it with girls from different walks of life, parts of Scotland and different ages. We all had something in common – we all had some problems with our brains. The staff in there were nice too, although I still hold them partially responsible for the state of my left eye. On the other hand, they were very helpful and attentive. In the most embarrassing situations for me, they were very understanding and discreet, no matter what their age or sex. My long stay there positively influenced our rapport. We became very friendly towards one another, for example they knew I hated bed baths and therefore I had a shower every day. Unfortunately two girls passed away during my stay and some were sent to other institutions. My husband was with me every step of the way; however, I will elaborate about him, my family and friends a wee bit later.

After ten and half months, I moved to a care home (CH), where I spent another seven months. You could say that it was a long time, however in terms of the care home it was a short stay. It is very close to my previous flat and our current home, which we own. My time in the nearby CH was not so scary, as my health was much better and I was on the way to recovery. So much so, that I moved there in April and around June had the PEG removed – literally torn out of my belly.

I was a resident of a Less Complex Care unit – one of four units in the entire CH. Despite all my issues with my health, I was the healthiest resident there. The staff there were nice too. They made sure that they knew our (other residents' and mine) routines and were able to anticipate our needs. There were a few carers who really 'went the extra mile' for me.

I used to get up soon after the change to day staff, which was just after eight a.m. After toilet, shower and breakfast I would come back to my bed with the exception of lunch time. At three p.m. I would join the staff for coffee and a blether. Between 4:30 and 5:00 p.m. our dinners would be served. After that my husband would come to visit me. I would go to sleep around 9:30-10 p.m. My stay there helped me to recuperate more and get me and my husband ready for our new life ahead.

I came back home fully on 4th December 2017, which was almost one year and seven months after I went to the hospital for the first time. At first, my routine at home was very similar to the one in the CH. After my morning personal care and breakfast, my new home carers would put me back to bed and I would listen to music or snooze until lunchtime. After lunch, I would go back to bed until my husband came back from his work, or I would go away for some exercise, initially two to three times a week. I used to go back with my home carers to my old CH, for a free of charge exercise bike for disabled people and a coffee and chat with my 'old' carers. This has continued for over a year, until we eventually bought our own recumbent exercise bike at home, so I could strengthen my legs at home more often. I also had weekly NHS physiotherapy appointments for over a year, where I had been strengthening my body and learning how to walk again.

After a month, I had come back home for good and I started to watch TV again. I had lots of spare time on my hands, so you could say I became addicted to it 'a little bit'. Netflix and Amazon Prime Video became my 'new friends'.

Some time ago, a few months after coming back home fully, I decided that I could not spend almost all day in bed. Therefore, I started to watch TV instead of going back to bed after lunch. Then, I decided not to go back to bed during the whole day, like other adults. I would watch TV all day, starting after my morning visits until my husband came back from his work with a break for my lunch visit. After some time, I got bored with only watching TV. Between my morning and lunch visits, to exercise my mind more, I started to play 'Sudoku' instead. Also, I started to follow celebrities and some series on Instagram (it is called 'my addiction'). Eventually, I got bored with this and came back to TV. Currently, I do other things but more about them later ...

2
My childhood and teenage years

Let me tell you about my life …

My parents told me that I was born on Sunday 5th June 1983 at 14:10 in my hometown of Lubartów in Poland and I believe this to be true. I was due on 14th June, but my brother was very sick and in hospital and I arrived earlier.

It is worth explaining at the beginning, that I am very bad with chronological dates and facts, especially as it was so long ago. This is why I have only focused on some of my memories from those times.

I think that I was very lucky because my childhood was very happy, full of fun, love and good memories. I had no drama, no 'creepy uncles' and no big trouble, just a normal 'life'.

There are four of us in my family, my parents, my brother (who is four years older than me) and me. My brother was my 'hero' when we were growing up, I wanted to be like him. When I was a little girl, I even tried to pee like him and I believed that we had the day off from nursery, school or work because of his birthday – in fact the 11th November is a national holiday in Poland, Independence Day. He wanted me to walk when I was a baby and dislocated both of my arms trying to stand me up. When we were a bit older, I had to be his goalkeeper at home or on the beach, responsible for getting the ball back of course. He was really obsessed with football, to the extent that I had to give him the random football results for his imagined league so he could find out the best team.

There are many more crazy stories about my brother but they will stay in my memory for now.

My parents are very loving and supportive towards me, they always were. Mum would make sure that the home was clean, we were clean, full and happy and our homework was done. She would patiently do what I expected of her. Like the time when I came back home and asked her to cut me some cucumber and give me a mirror. I lay down on the sofa and put pieces of cucumber on my face. After maybe thirty seconds I checked my face in the mirror and I realised that putting cucumbers on my face would not get rid of my freckles. Without any further delays I went back to play with my friends and never asked about the freckles again.

Dad would work a lot to be able to provide for his family. Sometimes, while Mum would take care of us, he would go to Germany to earn more money and bring back food and toys which were not available in communist Poland. I still remember the taste of cherry juice in small cartons, and the fact that I did not like bananas when I tried them for the very first time. I can still remember my first real Barbie in a pink and denim dress with long blonde hair and arms bent at the elbows like some kind of robot. I also got a babylike doll and played mums and kids with my friends from my block of flats. I would always be able to go on different trips and holidays in summer and in winter, both abroad and in Poland. There were also lots of family trips. We usually travelled by car and my dad promised that when were able to drive we would be able to listen to our own music. Later we learned that it would not be the case, we did not have a choice but listened to Enigma, Santana, Gypsy Kings and many more of the bands he liked. I cannot forget the taste of cold honeydew melon in Spain. It was so hot there and there was this melon and air conditioning in a restaurant where we had our dinner. It was an organised trip and we were travelling by bus. It was the first and the last time that we went on a family trip organised by someone other than my parents. We also had lots of family summer holidays in Hungary. I remember that once I was competing with three foreign boys on the water flume and I was celebrating my victory when I felt that something was wrong. It turned out that my swimsuit had fallen down and everything above my waist was revealed.

It was my dad who introduced me to the band Queen. It was 1st December 1991 and we were watching a TV programme about the life and death of Freddie Mercury when I asked my dad about this band. The next day he gave me a cassette of their music and I have been hooked ever since. Just before my brain haemorrhage, I went to see Queen and Adam Lambert live in concert in Glasgow.

My parents would always remember my birthday and other occasions, I was always given presents. I remember when my parents left ice skates for me in the night before the 6th of December, which is St. Nicholas' day in Poland, when you give and receive presents, and I was sleeping in them all night because I was so excited.

Mum is the oldest of three siblings. She has a younger sister and brother, my godfather (my first mobile phone was a present from him). Both her parents have already passed away. They were not that close to my brother and me, despite the fact that they stayed in my hometown. There is one thing I will never forget. For my eighteenth birthday, my maternal grandfather gave me cash and a plastic grapevine. At first, I thought it was very original idea, a grapevine instead of flowers. To my surprise, it turned out to be a plastic vine. I had a chuckle with my mum and I remembered that they used to have this fruit bowl full of plastic fruit. Do not ask me why!

As far as my dad's family is concerned, he is the middle child. He has an older brother and younger sister, my godmother (she always buys me lots of girly things as she has two boys). His father, my granny's first husband passed away a good few years ago and I do not remember her second husband as he passed away when I was very little. Our paternal grandfather (Granny's first husband) was also not that close to us. Nevertheless, I remember him doing scrambled eggs for us (my brother, our cousins and me) when we were children for breakfast every day at 6 a.m. when he was looking after us for a few weeks once during our summer holidays.

My paternal granny is still alive, although she is in a very fragile state. She was always around and took a very active part in our upbringing. I have lots of memories of her, but I will reminisce about just a few, as I could spend hours talking about her. My granny was living with us for some time and would always tell me stories about growing up during WWII, while we were eating dried pumpkin seeds and sitting in jammies in her bed in the morning. She would look after the four of us (my brother, our cousins, who were the children of my dad's older brother and me) when our parents were away together. Once, she threw a leather slipper at us, as we would not settle late in the night while she was watching TV. Me and her other granddaughter were given dolls in dresses in our favourite colours, from one of her many trips. We were both flat as pancakes when we were younger and we both complained about this a lot. One day, she spat on our chests and said some 'magic' words. The running joke is that it must have worked, as we are both chesty now, just like her.

The four of us would spend lots of time together when we were growing up, especially since we were similar ages. We decided one day that we would record a radio programme with my youngest cousin being responsible for the sport, as he was very funny.

During my childhood and teenage years, for a few weeks in the summer my other cousin would visit me. She is from my mum's side (the daughter of my mum's sister, from my auntie's first marriage) and I am only one year older than her. She actually lives far away from my hometown and for those few weeks we were inseparable. I can remember some of the many good stories with her. After my First Holy Communion, in the second year of primary school, in mainly Catholic Poland, I got some cash and bought myself a brand-new red BMX. My cousin was taking it for a spin and I was riding my brother's BMX, as it was better. She missed the turn and ended up hitting a lamp post. She also could not wait to become more chesty and she was very jealous of me, let just say that God/nature was very generous to her later on.

I was a very happy bunny at home and I loved school. When I started, if not for my parents and brother, I could have stayed in school all the time. I really liked my primary school, but not so fanatically in my older years. My best friend at school had the same name as me, she was known therefore as the 'Little One', as she was smaller than me. We sat together and did lots of different projects together, we were simply inseparable.

Our paths separated in high school (HS), when we joined classes with different orientations as I had chosen a class with more emphasis on maths, physics and IT. One of my besties till now (Olga) joined a second class with the same orientation as me, we knew each other from swimming and ski holidays. I had the pleasure of being her maid of honour at her wedding a few years ago. We see each other very rarely but when we meet it is like being back in HS.

It is same with one of my other best friends to this day (Teresa). I love this girl too with her dry sense of humour. Although we were in the same class in primary school, we became close in HS. Afterwards, she chose the IT path and to study in Warsaw, where she still lives and works.

HS was also the time when my brother fell into the wrong crowd and there were lots of arguments between him and my dad, with my mum stuck in the middle. At this time, I did not like to come back to my home.

I also have good memories concerning my eighteenth birthday party (in Poland this is a big deal). Although I had twisted my ankle before the party, I got permission to have a fun night and not to worry about it, as it would be treated again if needed.

I remember exactly what I was doing when 9/11 happened. We were doing a project with my friends from HS, in my home when I went to my living room to ask my dad something. He was watching the Polish version of *Who wants to be a millionaire*? Suddenly, the information showed in a 'Breaking News' strip. My dad changed the channel to CNN, where this tragedy was unfolding live. We initially thought that we were witnessing some movie being made.

I was very religious in PS and throughout HS. My upstairs neighbour, who recently passed away, used to say that I had a good chance of becoming a nun back then. Me, a nun? Impossible!

I finished HS with flying colours and passed my final exams very well.

Now there was time to go holiday without my parents for the first time in my life. I went to the Polish seaside with Olga, her older sister and their older cousin. We had a very good time and I was eventually ready to move away from home ...

3
My studies in Poland

After my holidays at the Polish seaside I was ready to begin my studies in Poznań, Poland, which is very far away from my home. It is worth mentioning that I had passed my entry exams, but I only just got into my university (the University of Economics). Later, I had good grades, although the beginning of my university life was quite hard, harder than I had anticipated initially. The huge distance between me and my family; my grades, not like those at HS; and the lessons on the value of money meant I was struggling. At first, my mum was saying that it was just a matter of time that I would look for excuses not to come home.

I went to university with a friend from HS (Emilia). We were not as close during high school. She had and still has a nickname after one of the characters from *The Addams Family* due to her hairstyle and clothing then. Sharing a room and being completely lonely in the new city brought us closer together. In the third year I was partying a lot, however not with her. This was because she had a boyfriend, with whom I had good conversations. We are still close friends, however, we are not 'BFFs'.

At first, we were sharing a flat with a girl with the same name, although she was older than us. It was funny when someone called and asked to speak to 'Magda' we all would ask, "Which one?". The oldest of us was very much into salsa, amongst her other hobbies and I would tag along with her from time to time. In our third year, she decided to start living with her boyfriend and she moved out from the flat we all were sharing. I also remember that I was told that I looked like I could be a shot putter by some random drunk, once when I was traveling home from my university.

We got a new flatmate then. She was also older than us, in her last year, already working. She was travelling lots for work that is why we were calling her room, 'Room for Hours'. We lived together just for one year but these were funny and crazy times. She and her group of friends accepted us straight away, like we had all known one another for years. We even formed a kind of alliance (together4ever), but unfortunately it has not stood the test of time. It was also her who introduced us (Emilia and me) to Michael Bublè, whose music I have simply loved since then.

In my third year, two years after me, Teresa's younger sister (Julia) also moved to Poznań, for her studies at the University of Medicine and she was living in the students' hall near to our flat. We became close as I took her under my wing, as I knew exactly what it meant to be new to the city. One of many memories I have of her is listening to George Michael's song *I can't make you love me* and *Tell Him* by Barbara Streisand and Celine Dion.

I loved to listen to these songs because I had a big crush on this boy. It started in my third year and lasted around twelve months. He was from a different specialisation but we had some lecturers together and we both were part of two different friend circles partying together. I can still remember *Sing Hallelujah* and *Time of my life*, playing very often in the student clubs, like Exam, where we were partying every Tuesday and sometimes even twice a week. As previously mentioned, I had a crush for around a year but I never admitted that to him or his group of friends. I also remember when I got a yellow and pink rose from him for my birthday. My birthday party was in the usual spot with the usual crowd. At the same party, I was dancing on the table, then later I was sleeping on it, as I had mixed my flu meds with alcohol.

There were two other girls in the same situation, one of my besties till now (Phoebe) and her cousin (Zosia), they had a 'silent' (they also did not admit it) crush too. We used to call them (crushes) by the abbreviation MBA, which was the running joke as we were studying at the International Relations faculty and therefore it was relevant to our studies. I had a crush on ‘M’ Phoebe on ‘B’ and Zosia on ‘A’. I remember that one time, I was very embarrassed. We were exchanging yellow post notes about it during a lecture with my Master Thesis Mentor who mentioned it at the end of his speech to the entire audience.

As mentioned before, I was partying a lot in my third year of studies. During this time, I unfortunately wasted my parents’ money and failed my language exam in Advanced English. The winter exams session in my third year was also very eventful. I received my first 2 (I failed my exam in the subject of Corporate Finance) and my first and only 6 (the highest possible grade for the History of Economic Thought). I must say that failing this exam gave me some good times and memories. Emilia and Phoebe’s cousin passed it and went home to enjoy their winter break, whereas Phoebe moved in with me for that period of time. There were quite a few of us who had to resit this exam. We had our own study group, consisting of people we knew very well and one guy who passed the exam but stayed to help us to understand and learn it. It was a very good week full of studying together, helping one another and lots of laughter. I also remember Phoebe cutting her own hair with thinning scissors above the toilet in my flat, one evening after group studies.

At the beginning of my studies I was close to Zosia as we were in the same group, but with time my bond with Phoebe started to grow and tighten up. I will never forget one of first things she said to me. She said that I should have some radio programme after 11p.m., because of the tone of my voice. We became besties, she was even my maid of honour at my wedding. Our friendship flourished over the years but I will elaborate about this a little bit later, when describing different parts of my life, as our paths intertwined with each other.

It is worth mentioning that I changed flat in my fourth year. The owner of our old flat decided to sell it, therefore we had to move out. After the holidays in London, I moved to Phoebe’s and Zosia’s flat, for a short period of time until

I found myself a new place. Emilia moved to her auntie firstly, then she stayed with me in my new room for over a month (she had an apprenticeship in a company, one of my new flatmates was working for at the time) and she found herself a new room eventually. My new room was in a flat, which I shared with three other girls. In the beginning, it was strange but we got very well on with one another eventually, to the extent that we would all watch TV together and drink hot mulled wine with oranges at Christmas time. One of them even helped me with the preparations for my trip to London in March. 'Our Devil' (nickname – explained later) also visited me in Poland and admitted to having a crush on my old roommate Emilia, but it was not mutual.

I used to spend my summer holidays in London, starting with summer 2004 and the last time in the summer of 2006. In April 2004 Poland joined the EU and Poles were able to work legally in the UK. My dad bought me and Emilia bus tickets (yes, bus tickets – the 'cheap' flights did not exist back then) for the beginning of summer, therefore we had to pass all our exams on earlier dates (called in Poland – 'zerówka'). My godfather's wife's sister took care of us in London. What was meant to be our accommodation just for the beginning, turned out to be our place to stay till the end of summer (we shared a flat with her and her three female flatmates) and then it was the time for us to come back for our third year of studies. When I was leaving for London, I had short red hair, it was even shorter and blonde with black spots (yes, I looked like a cow, although I did not see it that way back then) when I came back. We became very close to a couple of Italians, one of whom was training to be a hairdresser.

My first and only job that summer was in a coffee shop with a blue and black logo. At first Emilia helped me, as I was having troubles with my English but then I was called 'chatter box' during my interview. We had our formal training together but after the training on the job, we were placed in different coffee shops. My place of work was on Tottenham Court

Road, but it does not exist anymore as the centre of London has changed so much over the years. This coffee shop was open till 12:30 a.m. on Fridays and located near Soho, therefore it was quite busy. I became friends with an English guy with the nickname 'Our Devil'. When we worked together, we would play a game in front of customers, when he would ask me, "Magda, who is the best striker?" and I would shout back "Alan Shearer", as he was a big fan of Newcastle FC at the time. I really have lots of good memories from that holiday, it was a very hot and eye-opening summer.

My second time in London was the summer of 2005, between the third and fourth year of my studies. This time I went with Teresa and Olga; unfortunately after three weeks Teresa decided to go back home. We found scary accommodation (the building was very old and full of mice, who were very 'brave' especially in the night; the guy serving the never-changing breakfast looked dead – he had a very pale complexion) but it was very cheap (most importantly). I came back to my old place of work and I was told that my old manager had left and his assistant had been promoted and had his own coffee shop in Curzon Street in Mayfair. I went there and the manager recognised me straight away from the previous year and promised to speak to the area manager (the same guy from the previous year, both of them were from Italy).

I also remember the morning of the bombings in London. Olga and I had heard about the first bomb on the radio but we thought that someone had just got very angry. That morning London simply stopped. There was no public transport, no communications. We were kept in some kind of 'silent' bubble to prevent the panic, I guess. People outside London knew much more than we did in London. I eventually managed to get in touch with my family and friends to let them know that I was ok.

After a few days I started in a coffee shop in Mayfair although I was told at my first meeting that the manager there already had enough staff (it turned out that someone had been moved to a different location in order for me to join this shop, as both managers were very happy with the way I had worked the year before). Over the course of the summer, I became friendly with all the staff, boys and girls from different countries and regular customers. I even liked one person from the staff (Ali) more. The feeling was mutual, as it turned out. Only a week before my planned departure he admitted to me he liked me and wanted me to stay in London with him. I knew that it was not possible unfortunately. Because of my unfinished studies and his nationality and religion my parents would not approve of my decision to stay. The last week of my stay in London that summer was extremely nice, as no one, apart from our loved ones/close friends, no one knew that we were seeing each other. Not seeing a future, we both decided that it would be better not to stay in close contact with each other, when I was back in Poland.

It should be said that the beginning of my fourth year was difficult for me and I had to find myself new accommodation too. As previously mentioned, I found it. In December, Ali and I started to talk over the phone again, quite a lot actually as it was very hard for both of us to move on. It was quite funny to notice that the guy I had had a crush on during my third year, was a bit surprised by me paying less attention to him.

I mentioned previously that one of my new flatmates helped me with the preparations for my London trip in March. It was to visit Ali. After this trip I wanted to study in London, I even got Phoebe to go with me, but university fees and the cost of living in London were too high. Therefore, Phoebe and I decided to follow my old roommate and went for studies in Scotland, but I will elaborate about it later.

My third and last summer in London was between my fourth year and the studies in Scotland. My parents were not very happy that I chose to go back to London (especially as my dad was against my relationship with a Muslim; I still find it quite bizarre, taking into account how Polish men treat Polish women as well) instead of Dundee (where I was to study). I went there with Olga and Emilia, but after some time the first of the girls decided to go back home. We stayed in a hostel found by Ali. I could not get back to the coffee shop in Mayfair, as there was a 'couples not able to work together' policy and they got to know it by coincidence. Ali was very private about his personal life at work; however, it was me in March after the closing of the coffee shop, who shared with some guy that I had worked at that place a year earlier. They checked the recording tape and were very angry that I did not pop in and say 'hi' and see them. I even had a theory that another Polish girl, who also was working with us, secretly liked Ali too, but the feeling was not mutual. Instead, I used to work in a shop nearby to my hostel that sold coffees and freshly made sandwiches and salads at first, but after two weeks the manager (Polish guy trying to convince others he was native, who also had a serious drinking problem) lost it after his assistant simply walked away and he fired me and another junior staff member. I have heard that this place burnt down soon after.

Ali helped me to find a new job, actually it was two (because there were not enough hours from one). The morning one was in a coffee shop at Paddington train station. It paid my bills but I disliked this job. There were mostly three things which really bugged me. First of all, the time I was starting most of my shifts – 6 a.m., secondly all these pigeons tried to grab partially unfinished chunks of sandwiches, muffins or pastries. I also hated one of the French girls, who was my supervisor. She would always open the dishwasher during its cycle so then the person washing the dishes would have to start again and she thought that she was better than us. My second job as a waitress was in a restaurant run mostly by Albanians with Polish chefs. I worked there some afternoons and I liked this job more. Unfortunately, I did not manage to save for my future studies (as planned earlier), but I had great last holidays in London.

At the end of summer, we (Emilia and I) went back home for two weeks, before starting our studies in Scotland.

4
My studies and life in Scotland till my 'trip' to hospital

I was in my fifth and final year of my studies in Poland, when I went to study abroad. My Polish university had an arrangement with a Scottish university in Dundee (the University of Abertay, Dundee). My grades were transferred and I was able (free of charge studies for all EU students, apart from English students) to start my fourth year there concluding in the title of Bachelor of Arts with Honours. I had decided earlier that I would like my Scottish grades to be transferred back to my Polish university. This meant that I was able to finish my studies in Poland, while studying abroad. It is worth mentioning here again that the studies in Scotland were not my first choice. I wanted to study in London, I also got accepted for one semester onto 'Erasmus' (student exchange programme) in France. However, due to economic reasons (I was able to work legally in the UK, as I had not managed to save during my last summer in London) and a chance of getting a diploma, I decided to study in Scotland.

It was actually Emilia who brought the possibility of studying in Scotland to my attention. There were quite a few of us (students from my Polish university), who decided to study there as well at the same time. Emilia, Phoebe, her cousin (she was at Erasmus in Lithuania on the second semester of our fourth year and decided during her online chat with Phoebe to apply for the same university as us) and I shared a two-bedroom flat. I shared a bedroom with Emilia, the other two girls with each other and we would swap rooms after six months. We all got jobs eventually (I knew that I could not expect my parents to cover all my expenses in Scotland, as studying abroad was my own idea). I used to work in one of many coffee shops in the centre of

Dundee, as my first job. There were lots of us from different countries in different stages of life. I met my close friend Rachel and we both had a feeling that we had known each other before. She is Polish too, but a year younger than me. We instantly became friends and still are to this day.

At the university we all were in the Business School, but in different faculties. I was the only one out of the four of us to choose Business Studies as my faculty at Scottish university. This meant that I did not have to write a dissertation, as I would be awarded my title just after getting my grades from the tutorials and passing the exams. The studies in Scotland were interesting because I had an opportunity to study with students from all over the world and foreign professors (as opposed to my flatmates, who were saying it was like studying in 'Little Poland'). I managed to pass my tutorials and exams quite well and therefore I was awarded my Upper Second-Class degree with Honours (BA Hons 2:1 in Business Studies).

The plan was to go back to Poland after one year and Emilia and Zosia stuck to it, but Phoebe and I decided to stay a bit longer (well, it will be fourteen years for me in September and I am not going anywhere). During that academic year I had my Polish graduation in May and my Scottish one in July 2007 (my parents were at my Polish one, although I was not yet awarded my Master's degree, that happened later).

It is worth mentioning that my long-distance relationship did not stand the test of time, despite the fact that we both visited each other on a couple of occasions. It definitely finished in February 2007, as we both were expecting from each other things we could not deliver. Ali contacted me later, when I was already in a relationship with my future husband, on a few occasions but I only remember two of them. The first one happened around two years into my relationship with my future husband, whom I told about the email (calling me for Islam) I had received and who reacted by saying something that I would not want to repeat. The second time was around two years later, I replied to the message saying that going into business together was a very bad idea taking into account our past together. Besides, I knew very well that my future husband would not be too chuffed if I decided otherwise.

During that academic year, I also became closer to Pepper. We used to study together in Poland, in different faculties though. She was actually the first one to get married (to Tony in April 2008 and they have a beautiful daughter) from my current circle of closest friends. I was alongside other Poles representing her side at the first Polish-Scottish wedding in our group of friends. Thanks to her help I was able to finish my Master's Thesis and obtain my Master's degree from my Polish university. She facilitated it so that I was able to use her employer as the example in my thesis titled 'Knowledge Transfer in the Multinational Corporation'. After her Scottish studies, she decided to stay here as well.

I also decided to stay in Scotland (as previously mentioned Phoebe decided that too) and I started to work in a bar in Dundee as well as in the coffee shop. I started to work there as I had more free time after finishing my studies and I needed more money. I eventually stopped working for the coffee shop and I worked full-time in the bar. In there I met my other close friend (Bruce). He actually took me for a drink across the street to a night club after my first shift in the bar. I still like gin with cranberry juice and a wedge of fresh lime, which he introduced me to. That was back in September 2007 and we have been friends ever since, he even calls me 'Babcia', which means 'Granny' in Polish. He has moved on from Hospitality and he joined the Police a few years ago and currently works and lives in Edinburgh (with his long-term girlfriend, Natasha). In the bar, I also quickly became friends with Sam (my supervisor) and George (a few years younger than me and on whom I had a little crush until I realised that he was still in 'the closet'). I really enjoyed working there, we would work hard but also party hard.

My parents were pressing me to come back home and finish my Master's Thesis, which despite enjoying my party lifestyle I knew myself I had to do. I eventually booked my ticket home but a week before my flight an office agency called saying that they had a temporary office position for me. I had been complaining to them that I really needed office experience as it had been very hard for me to get any. The position was starting in four days, so I decided to cancel my flight home to get the office experience I wanted.

As previously mentioned, Phoebe also decided to stay in Scotland. After the other girls left, Phoebe and I firstly moved in with her friend for two weeks, then we shared a flat (where we both shared a room) with her other friend from work (Chandler). After six months, his girlfriend moved in with us (Monica, my flatmates used to work with her) and she made us both wear bras under our pj's when we came to the living room not yet dressed (she admitted later that she was simply jealous).

I also remember that Phoebe and I decided to host a meal for a few Polish friends for Easter and both Monica and Chandler spent most of their Easter Sunday in the kitchen helping us, as lots of people turned up who were invited by our guests without our knowledge. We were also living for a while with Rachel and her flatmates, eventually just three of us renting out a flat. We thought that we were on the top of the world, as each of us had her own bedroom. In fact, this was a badly refurbished student flat. Rachel's room was in the shape of the letter C, with my room barging into hers and the wall between our rooms was very thin.

At that time I was already solely working for a finance company (FC). Let me explain how this happened. Back in February 2008 I started my temping job in the FC through the office agency. I knew that I needed office experience, no matter where I ended up. At first, I was coping quite well with both jobs, they were even impressed with my office performance, so much so I was told to apply for a permanent position. I did so and I became directly hired by the FC. Around a month earlier I decided to resign from my job in the bar, in order to focus more on my office career. I also knew that I had to write my Master's Thesis and I managed this with 'a little help from my friend' Pepper. I also took some time off from the FC, as I had an official deadline for writing my thesis and passing my final exam at the end of October 2008, otherwise I would have to repeat my studies from the beginning in order to be awarded a degree.

As previously mentioned, three of us (Phoebe, Rachel and I) moved in together and soon after that Julia started to live in the flat in the next close (she also came for a student exchange; this was two academic years after me again). We called her 'Marie' because she would come in, take her shoes off, then go to the kitchen, wash any dishes, and then she would make tea for everyone and join us. I used to help her with the coursework, dissertation (I would help with writing in English and check her work) and I managed to learn some new things, although we both were studying completely different subjects.

I have lots of memories from the time we lived in this flat. We held a Christmas party, where we invited lots of our friends and I very much ignored my future husband (who hardly knew anyone). We also had an amazing Christmas there. There were eight of us but Phoebe and her boyfriend at that time went to sleep earlier (he showed up very late for our special meal, because of his job and he was starting early the next day). Because we were all Poles, we had our traditional meal (celebrated in Poland on December 24, called 'Wigilia') and after midnight we opened wine and the fun started. It was a night full of funny games, jokes and laughter. It was already dawn when we finished our celebrations. Julia went to her flat, Rachel and I shared her bed, mine was occupied by Bruce and one of his flatmates (Tomasz, who lives in Poland now). Bruce's other flatmate (Bartosz who also went back to Poland) was sleeping on our living room floor (on a bed made of the cushions from the sofa).

This flat also 'saw' the beginning of my relationship with my future husband. I got to know Ross, Rachel's long-term boyfriend there as well. It is actually a funny story with his nickname which he got back then. One evening (at the beginning of their relationship) Rachel was sick but when she came back home from his, she was miraculously cured the next day so Ross gained the nickname 'Doctor'.

As mentioned previously, during the time we were renting our first flat together, I was still working at the FC. I met my very close friend Bernadette there for the very first time. We used to work in different departments and at the beginning we had heard of each other but neither of us was interested in the new colleague (just because we both are Polish). We were eventually assigned to the same project and we 'clicked' straight away. We are still very close, despite the fact that she lives with her own family (husband Howard, who she married in May 2008 and a beautiful daughter) on the other side of the world now. My friend Sam also joined the FC, on a temporary basis at first and was in another team but the same department as me.

I really liked my job at first. The team I was assigned to, including the manager, were very funny and cheeky to me. With time I built my knowledge and eventually became solely responsible for fees (I even called myself the 'fees monkey'). A new building, the reconstruction of the corporate structure and strategy did not bring the changes I was expecting (a pay rise and/or help with my job). They did not even want to put me through any qualifications, recognised by the industry (pensions related) either. I did not see any other option but to look for new opportunities elsewhere.

My new job was with another finance company (oFC) in their office in Dundee. Bernadette was also fed up with her job in the FC and also changed her employer to the same as me, in fact she started the new job a week before me. We became close with another of my closest friends, Penny. I had actually met her on a few occasions previously, however we did not study together, as she is one year older than me (same as Bernadette in fact). Firstly, Penny, who married Leonard back in October 2009 and they have a beautiful son, was our supervisor, however we both were eventually moved to different teams with new bosses. I even managed to call one of our direct client's representatives 'Satan' instead of 'Satien' during the weekly call and both of the teams reacted with a long pause and quiet chuckles on our side.

During my time in this company, Bernadette and I decided to try Flamenco. It was great fun but how to put it, we were not the greatest dancers. I also remember different teams competing in *Come Dine with Me.* It was great fun too, as some of our consecutive Fridays were filled with good food, alcohol and laughter. I remember that while working there I fell from the windowsill onto our bedroom floor and hurt my back a little (just muscles). Phoebe and my future husband called the ambulance, as I thought that I had broken my back. I was in such shock that I actually enjoyed the male first responder checking my back. It was then that my future husband got to know that he needed glasses. A few days after my little accident, my back was still very sore, which is why we drove to the hospital, where I could read from a nearby notice board but he was not able to.

After a few years I decided to move on with my career, therefore I looked for a new position and I managed to secure myself a job with an investment bank (IB) in Edinburgh.

I was already living with my future husband but let me explain this in some more detail. Back in August 2008, three of us (Phoebe, Rachel and I) changed our first flat together for a bigger one, in Dundee as well. Rachel had the biggest room that time, mine was a bit smaller and Phoebe had the smallest of the bedrooms. This time all the bedrooms, were shaped normally and we even had a dining area in our kitchen and a big living room. We stayed there for another year. We organised lots of different parties there, like a house warming party or a party for Phoebe's birthday/Halloween. We also decided to organise 'Wiglia' for around fifteen of us (different friends, who had also decided to stay in Scotland at that time) at Christmas as well as parties at Hogmanay and Easter. After sharing a flat with my friends, I decided I was ready for the next step in my relationship. As the result of a conversation that I had had with my future husband, we moved in together for the very first time. Phoebe decided to come back to Poland and for her last month in Scotland, she was staying with us. Rachel moved in with Bruce at that time.

We stayed in this flat in Dundee for a year and half and then moved to Linlithgow, from where he was commuting to work in Stirling and I was commuting to and from Edinburgh. We stayed till the end of lease on our second place in Linlithgow, I was already in the rehab hospital at that time.

As previously mentioned, I got a job in Edinburgh and we moved to Linlithgow. To be perfectly honest, I got a different job than the one I had applied for in the beginning. The IB decided that my previous experience from the other FC in Dundee (when I was at the team managed by Penny) would be of more benefit to them and I was hired for a position with the team dealing with Financial Forecasting (I was the only girl there). After two and half years of a very fast paced environment, I moved to a different team, with not such a fast pace. In the team dealing with transactions the dynamics were also different, as there only was one boy when I moved there. I worked there for a year, until December 2015 when my health issues started. Just before my bleed, I was looking for another job, as I really liked my manager on a personal level but I hated working with them, as they did not have a clue about our processes but it would seem that they had broad knowledge. I did not get the new position. There is a Polish saying that 'Fortunately there was some good in my bad luck', meaning that I did not get the new job, but in my current health situation, it was better to be employed permanently and not be on probation.

The bleed happened on Saturday late morning, 7th February 2015 and I was diagnosed two days later, on Monday morning after different tests and checks. On

Saturday, I started to have a huge headache, so big that I thought that my head would explode. My future husband called an ambulance and I was taken to a nearby hospital, as I was not able to keep down any painkillers and my headache was just humongous.

They decided to leave me overnight in the hospital with a suspicion of muscle damage in my neck. The next morning a doctor with more experience started his shift and tested me quickly by raising both of my legs up and I felt pain in my neck then. I was ordered a CT scan of my head. When they scanned my head for a second time (this time with a dye), I knew something was wrong but I was not expecting in a million years what happened next. My husband and I were told that I had a bleed in my brain and I would be sent to WGH in Edinburgh instead of home. I must say that it was a very big shock for both of us. I remember when I saw one of the girls in my ward in Edinburgh and I thought to myself that if I looked like that there would not be any wedding. On Monday morning I was eventually diagnosed with an AVM (I used to call it 'Sławek', a random male Polish name) on my brain stem, which had caused the bleed. One of the consultants from the DCN (Department of Clinical Neuroscience in the WGH) told me (after diagnosis) that I was actually lucky that the bleed was outside and not inside my brain.

It was me who had to inform my own family about my brain bleed and what had caused it. I must admit that it was the worst phone call I ever had to make, as I knew they would be worried sick even though I was calling them in person. After a few days in the DCN, I came back home, where I recovered further. I was away from my work for a total of two weeks.

I came back to work on a phased return basis at first. Later, at the end of April and the first two weeks of May I was off work because of my surgery, after which I returned there on a phased basis too.

It is worth mentioning that I was ordered not to fly because of the issues with my brain. In July I got married and afterwards we had our driving honeymoon. After the check up in October everything seemed to be quite well. Little did I know what the future was holding for me.

At the beginning of December, I started to have dizziness. At the beginning, they (in my GP's practice in Linlithgow) thought that it was an ear infection, as my friend from work had it too but hers was gone after a few weeks. I started to be very impatient with my GP and demanded to be referred to an ENT specialist as I had my private medical insurance (in my opinion they should have had me marked as a high-risk patient due to my health issues with my brain). It was actually my mum who convinced me to contact my neurologist, who at first advised that it (my dizziness) could not be related to my brain issue. Nobody expected that in fact. I saw this ENT specialist and I was ordered to get a special MRI scan, as he would do nothing before getting the results, because of my previous issues. I had this special scan and on 8th January 2016 I started to take steroids from my neurologist, as it turned out that my dizziness was caused by a brain swelling where I had had my surgery at the end of April 2015.

I was not able to commute or work in my usual fast-paced environment but I could run the house. I became very domesticated, like never before. I was cleaning the whole house, washing and ironing all the clothes, cooking healthy meals and baking healthy snacks. I would make sure that all the housework was done and snacks prepared by Friday, so I could spend the weekend with my husband. He simply loved it and the roles are quite reversed now. I was able to walk with a stick (like an old granny), however by mid-April, even that proved to be very challenging and therefore I decided to stay at home. My mum then came to help but after a week or so my balance was very off. I could not even walk to the bathroom and therefore I was admitted to hospital on Tuesday 10th May 2016.

5
My husband

It was not love at first sight, actually the opposite. I met my husband (Misio) in the finance company in Dundee. The first time I saw him, I thought to myself, "Man, get a haircut", as he had long, centre-parted gelled hair. He was away from the office for a fortnight or so and when he came back, I did not recognise him at first, as he had actually had a haircut. That afternoon I came back home and said to my flatmates (Phoebe and Rachel) that it was amazing how a haircut could change a person.

I was temping in his team and he was showing me the different processes, I was helping with fees specifically. I started to like his way of thinking and he was getting my sense of humour. With time, I became more confident and even asked one day what I had to do to be part of his team, he responded by saying that I had to apply for a permanent position. I explained that I had meant simply to get him to make me a coffee too, when it was his turn. After that he started to make me coffee, although I was sitting in a different bank of desks, while on a temporary contract. I started to like him that way in April 2008, around the time of my successful application for a permanent role in the FC. I did nothing until December of the same year, when I decided to invite him to our Christmas party. Besides, I knew that he really liked this other girl (we were working together and I was quite close with her), but that feeling was not mutual. Bernadette and Sam knew that I liked Misio, but they both swore secrecy.

My husband is the youngest of three siblings. His sister is three years older than him and lives nearby, like the rest of the family actually. She is married to Peter and they have two beautiful children. My husband's niece is nine and a bit years old and his nephew is seven years old. My husband

and his brother, who is six years older than him, are the godparents of this nephew. Misio's brother does not have his own family, therefore works a lot. They also have a foster brother, who will have his big thirtieth birthday this year and he lives and works in Glasgow. My husband's parents are both retired and spend their time taking care of their grandchildren (up to three times a week) and looking after their garden (when it is warmer) or simply relaxing and reading/watching TV (in the winter). In my husband's family there is the rule of three – there are three years between siblings and between both parents. In my family there is the rule of four – my dad is four years older than my mum and I am four years younger than my brother.

You could say that I am a 'cougar' as my 'toy boy' husband is ten months younger than me. Therefore, I prefer it when he wears a beard, without which he looks too young in my opinion.

As previously mentioned, I liked my future husband from the time I got accepted by the FC for a permanent role but I did nothing till December, at that Christmas party. I completely ignored him during the party but I decided that I still liked him the next morning (he stayed over but nothing happened). We went for the very first coffee on Sunday 18th January 2009 and we have been together ever since. However, it was me who made the first move. Two days earlier in the late afternoon, I had sent him a text message, in which I had been very explicit about the way I had felt about him. I had not received any response till the next day, late afternoon as well. I had been already thinking about how to backtrack from my message on Monday morning, as I had wanted things to stay the same at least. The response eventually had came and it had turned out that the feeling had been mutual (the text message had even been in Polish). I also remember that in the evening of my first coffee with my future husband, I met my friend Sam and we even practised kissing, as I was scared that I had forgotten how to do it.

At the beginning of our relationship we only told a few at the FC about us being an item. More people knew about it, they were not thinking that it would last long and here we are having just celebrated our fifth wedding anniversary. In April of the same year, I met his entire family during his birthday meal (I knew it would be ok, when they welcomed me and said “Oh, so you do exist!” or when my husband’s dad said to my husband’s sister that they must know her because they had prepared two glasses for her) and it was very sweet when he got a CD and book to study Polish from his parents (he never looked into it, apart the time that he and his mates tried to read it for a laugh).

Misio met my family in parts. He met my dad back in May, when he visited me. My future husband then took us for different trips around Scotland. He met the rest of my family in the same year, in July. We went to Poland for my cousin’s wedding and my parents organised my ‘Name day’ party (it is very important to mention that it was my first ever party for this occasion). My future husband drank a lot and mixed alcohol (he wanted to prove that he could handle it) and vomited in my parents’ toilet.

My cousin’s wedding was the first Polish wedding he had attended. He eventually started to like the attention he was receiving because of his kilt (my aunt’s drunk hairdresser was even trying to check if he had boxers on under it). I must say that we had some Polish weddings every year till our own one. The year after Misio’s first wedding in Poland, we were guests at Monica’s and Chandler’s weddings in Scotland and Poland. I used to live with them and we were already close friends, so when Misio appeared in my life, he joined my circle of friends. He met Monica and Chandler at that Christmas party and they have been friends since then. I am also the godmother to their oldest daughter (they actually have two beautiful daughters, the oldest who just turned seven and the younger one who is two and a bit years old). From the many memories I have from that wedding, there is one I have to mention. After midnight I was not feeling well and I went to the toilet (basically I drank too much). I was very discreet about it (only Phoebe and my future husband knew), but when I came back to the party, even the bride's mum knew about my 'issues'. It turned out that my future husband had told everyone about my temporary indisposition and two hours later, we had to go back to our room as he had to go to sleep.

After a year and a half, we moved to our first flat in August 2010 just after our trip to Poland, for Monica's and Chandler's wedding. Phoebe stayed in our flat, as previously mentioned. Winter (we did not have any central heating, just electric heaters) was very bad then, to the extent that the whole of Scotland was paralysed. The snow was so bad that we missed the birthday meal for his mum's sixtieth. Also, my future husband was staying with his parents (it was closer and more convenient for him for his work) for a few days, while I was staying alone in our flat. I had a big knife and an orange on our bedside table, just in case. I kept the orange as the reason for having the knife in the bedroom, as had been advised earlier by Pepper's husband, Tony. Misio was the main cook there, he also had to listen to my moans about my job in the other finance company. On Saturdays (especially when *The X Factor* was on TV), Rachel (she was already living with Ross in a nearby flat to ours) would always pop in for a blether.

While living in our first flat, we went to another Polish wedding. This time it was my friend's, in October 2011. My old roommate Emilia and my parents were also guests at that wedding. This same year but during the summer months we went to Poland first and to Paris with Phoebe. Only Phoebe and I, amongst other friends, were invited to our friend's wedding.

I have many memories from our French trip, some of which need mentioning here, as they concern Misio. First of all, he did not listen to my advice about the suitcase before our trip. His suitcase did not have a decent handle and we all (Phoebe, Misio and I) had to take turns and pull his heavy luggage on our way to the hotel. Secondly, Misio slipped and fell when taking a shower one afternoon and I locked the door as I thought that someone was fighting outside. Another story concerns his knowledge of the French language. One morning, we (Misio and I) were responsible for buying some pastries for breakfast. He said that he would deal with it in the shop because he used to study French at school. The lady behind the counter asked him something in French and he agreed. It turned out that we bought decent sized croissants and the smallest ever pain au chocolat.

After eighteen months, we moved from Dundee to Linlithgow. Misio said that he would not move to Edinburgh, where I had got my new job with the IB, as it would mean a long commute for him again (he works in Stirling and drove every day there from Dundee). Therefore, we had to find another solution to this matter. We literally looked at the train line between Stirling and Edinburgh and that is how we got Linlithgow. We checked the town's website and decided that it would be our next place to stay in. We both liked this little but beautiful town, especially the ruins of Linlithgow Palace above the lake and nature walks there. It simply was a nice and relaxing place to unwind after commuting to and from busy cities (by train for me and by car for Misio).

First of all, we were renting the flat, which was three minutes away from the train station, which was perfect for me. We also had Tesco and my gym nearby. It was a gym for girls only (before turning the big three zero, I had decided that it had been high time to take care of my health and appearance) and I loved it. Five times a week, I was not only getting my exercise, but also girly chat, which I lacked at home (living with Misio only) and at work (working with boys only at that time). While living in this flat, we went to another wedding in Poland, it was my other cousin's wedding (the same cousin, who had visited me during the summer holidays when we had been both much younger). At that wedding I saw my uncle (auntie's second husband and bride's stepdad) for the last time, as he passed away after a long battle with pancreatic cancer. At the same wedding, Misio got drunk very quickly (everyone wanted to drink vodka with the man in a kilt and he was drinking with everybody). Thanks to my parents, my mum's side of the family and their friends, I still had a good time and even caught the bride's bouquet (Misio did not see that obviously, because he was sleeping in the kids' room with small furniture). After this wedding the four of us (my parents, Misio and I) went on holiday to Kraków (famous Polish city), after which Misio and I flew to London and then to Scotland.

For my thirtieth birthday Misio took me to London to see Michael Bublè live in concert for the first time ever (this was at the beginning of July 2013). In August the same year, we also went for holidays with my parents to the nearby lake (close to my hometown). Misio and I were also guests at my other cousin's wedding (we were the only guests because my parents and the bride's parents, meaning my dad's brother and his wife, have not spoken to one another for years now) and we really liked the venue (we had our wedding at the same venue). In fact, we had a good time with the bride's brother and his girlfriend (at the time) and also my very close friend Teresa and her boyfriend (at the time).

In January 2014, we celebrated our five years together with a fancy meal and Misio surprised me and asked me to marry him. I was over the moon obviously and agreed to his proposal. My parents were very happy, when I called them with this news on the same evening. We informed his parents the next day in person by showing my hand with my engagement ring. They could not hide their positive emotions. We then decided to share it with closer and further friends (I even facetimed Phoebe and Bernadette to show them my ring, without saying anything and waiting for their reactions). We both shared this news with our work colleagues as well.

In March/April 2014 we went to Australia to do a little bit of sightseeing and to meet friends who had emigrated there in September 2013. It is worth mentioning that together with Penny and Bernadette's other friend, we organised a surprise leaving party for Bernadette and her husband Howard and Misio helped me a lot. We had a great time in Australia and visited Sydney, Melbourne, Great Ocean Road (in reverse though) and Adelaide. One day, while travelling from Sydney to our friends, we had three breakfasts. The first one was at the airport in the early morning (we thought that we would not get it later). The second one was served on our flight to Adelaide. The third one was more like a feast, prepared by my very close friend Bernadette to welcome us to their new home. Later that evening, we even got a cake to celebrate our engagement. It is worth mentioning that our other close friends (Penny and Leonard) were visiting Adelaide at that time too. I also remember that we were told not to drive in Kangaroo Island after dusk. We (Bernadette and her husband, Misio and I and their little daughter) understood that quickly, when we were driving to our accommodation and we must have hit 93 kangaroos, attracted by the lights of our car. It is worth mentioning as well that Misio celebrated his thirtieth birthday while in Melbourne and we went to see Kevin Bridges at a comedy festival there. Our Australian adventure left us both really liking life there and really wanting to go back there someday.

After this Australian trip, we were guests at Monica's and Chandler's first daughter's christening and I became her godmother. We were late because of me and Misio had to drive very fast and the police stopped us. He earned three points on his license and we had to pay a £100 fine.

The same year, but in August, we went back to Poland for our sixth Polish wedding. Three of us (Rachel and us, unfortunately not Ross as well) flew directly to Poznań for Tomasz's and Anna's wedding (many of our friends from Scotland were also there). Phoebe was staying with us in the flat organised by the bride. Afterwards, Misio and I travelled to my hometown to visit my family.

Misio and I were very happy with our first flat in Linlithgow until the time our landlord was very reluctant to buy a new washing machine for almost a month, when the old one broke. We started to look for a new place. We had a viewing but the house was too small for us. We had another viewing. I simply fell in love with this house (very spacious bedrooms and good-sized garden; we really missed an outdoor space in the old flat) although it was above the monthly rent that we could afford. Long story short, the landlord agreed to decrease the monthly rent but we had to sign a contract for two years and he refurbished the house and I was even asked to choose the colours of the rooms. We moved there in September, just after our trip to Poland.

The beginning of 2015 was actually not bad at all. Misio took me to Glasgow to see Queen and Adam Lambert live in concert (that was in January) and a few days later he took me for my flight to Poland to see my family.

When I was taken to the nearby hospital with a headache and they left me in overnight with the suspicion of muscle damage in my neck, my husband simply thought that I was a hypochondriac. Therefore, he was shocked when they said that I had the brain bleed and would be sent to Edinburgh instead of home. My husband informed my work and our friends about my condition. He was strong for me; even calming down my brother, who travelled from Southern England after receiving my phone call, to check on me. Misio took the responsibility for my brother's stay and schedule of friends' visits to the hospital I was staying in. He also dealt with keeping everyone who was interested informed about my situation (my work, his family and friends living outside Scotland) and took time off his job to be with me in the hospital and look after me later, when I came back home before returning to work. He also had time off for my surgery at the end of April.

We received an invitation to another wedding in Poland (Bartosz's and Kamila's), but I had an order not to fly and therefore we did not go. Our own wedding was the seventh one (in Poland), as promised by Misio to my auntie (my mum's sister). He drove from Scotland to my hometown in

Poland. This epic journey took us three days because of the stops for sleep. On Friday we boarded the party boat in Newcastle, an overnight ferry to Amsterdam. On Saturday we managed to get to Western Poland and on Sunday we reached our destination. Due to my brain issues all preparations regarding my appearance on the day were left for the last week. My fiancé had his outfit ready and I only had shoes. It is worth mentioning that my parents, especially my mum, were on the top of all wedding preparations, even regarding me and my outfit (I felt like I had a wedding planner).

My fiancé and I decided to invite mostly our close families and friends. Because the wedding was in Poland (he did not want a wedding party in Scotland too) you would be right in thinking that there were more guests from my side but I still had my own 'tartan army'. I asked Misio's family and our Scottish friends to wear kilts if possible (my old roommate was even laughing that because of the kilts it would be a very different wedding in our hometown, with curious spectators). My fiancé's family stayed in wooden houses near to Lake Firlej (around 12 km from my hometown), which was close to the wedding venue and they treated the trip like a holiday, as the weather was very nice.

As previously mentioned, I had only a week to the Big Day. My wedding dress was ready in three days (on Monday the lady took my measurements for the very first time and it was ready on Friday morning) and my trial makeup and hairdo were on Wednesday. We got married on Sunday 15th July 2015 which was my dad's sixtieth birthday. The party flew by too fast and the next day Misio and I completely let go and got drunk, especially him (I must admit that you do have much more fun when you are just a guest at the wedding). Our separate wedding photo shoot with some landscapes in the background was on Wednesday, a few days after the wedding (which is tradition in Poland) and I would have changed that now, as it required me to put my dress back on and do my special makeup and hair again.

Our honeymoon started on Friday, when we travelled (Misio was driving again) to Budapest. We spent two days only there and after the F1 Hungarian Grand Prix on Sunday evening (it was actually my second time at the Hungarian Grand Prix, the first time I was there it was back in 1998 with my dad) we travelled to Prague. We spent a few days there but we both regretted leaving Budapest too early, as we both liked it more than Prague, however we had everything planned and booked. From Prague we travelled to Amsterdam, where we also spent a few days. I made my husband visit the 'Red Light District' a good few times, as I was really fascinated with it. After few days in Amsterdam, we bordered an overnight ferry to Newcastle and on Saturday afternoon we came back home to Linlithgow.

In August we both went to Glasgow to see Paulo Nutini in concert and we paid £100 to get back to Linlithgow. It was late and no way to get to the train station on time. We were trying our friends living there but we were not able to reach anyone and decided to take a taxi directly home instead of staying at some hotel and having to travel the next morning.

It is worth mentioning that Penny and Leonard had already moved to Edinburgh a good few months before and we all spent time together and became very close friends. In the beginning of October, they came to visit us during our last normally able holidays in Western Scotland (Wemyss Bay Caravan Park).

In October I had a check-up with my neurologist and all seemed to be fine. How little my husband and I knew about the changes which would happen later and completely reshape our life together. When I started to be dizzy in December, my husband was very supportive. He was worrying about me and always took me for different tests and checks. Until I was healthy enough (my dizziness was bearable and I was able to walk by myself), my husband and I would visit Penny and Leonard and their newborn son a lot (I realised that I have been sick all his life and he is almost five).

My husband simply loved it when I was staying at home, not because I was sick, but because I became a very domesticated wife. When I was hospitalised in WGH at first, he would visit every day after his work in Stirling or spend weekends in the hospital with me. It was the same when I was moved to the different hospital (rehab for brain). In fact, whichever hospital I was staying in, Misio would always visit me. For almost eleven and a half months I was hospitalised in Edinburgh, and there were only two occasions when my husband did not visit me, as he was that sick and it would be very dangerous for him to drive to Edinburgh (it was around forty miles one way).

He was there for me, even when I was literally crazy and was calling him ‘a traitor’. He also was trying his best (he was cooking a fattened soup and liquid Nutella with bananas) to make sure that I stayed off the feeding tube, however I eventually had it installed.

It was actually my husband, who changed the house we were renting in Linlithgow to a house in Tullibody, which was much more suitable for me in a wheelchair. My husband decided to move somewhere suitable for me and closer to his family (they all live in Clackmannanshire) in the situation that we were in. He was also making the decisions about my transfer to the care home, nearby to our previous and current accommodation. He visited me there every day, after his work (my care home was much closer than the rehab hospital in Edinburgh; it was just around nine miles one way).

In June/July 2017, we and my parents went on a week’s holiday to Dumfries. It was our first holiday in the new reality, as at that time I was still in the care home. I would come home for the weekends but it was my first trip as a disabled person. The same year but at the end of August, we decided to change our accommodation, as the house my husband was renting in Tullibody was not accessible for me in the long term (I was not able to easily access the first floor). We found a flat in Alloa (Clackmannanshire) next to the train station, where we stayed for two and a half years (although I fully came back home in the beginning of December, a few months after we started to rent it). This flat was very appropriate for my needs, those of a person confined to a wheelchair.

After I fully came back home, the roles reversed and my husband took over looking after the home, on top of his work. I would have carers coming to help me with my morning routine (bed stretches, toilet, shower, clothes, meds and breakfast), they would then show up for my afternoon visit too (lunch, toilet, three different exercise devices, refresh and change of the top, toilet). Then I would watch TV and wait for my husband to come back home from his work. He would then look after me in the evening. It is important to mention here that I required more care at the beginning of my stay at home but got better with time at being home alone.

My first flight, after getting the green light for flying, was to Belfast to the American embassy to get my visa for our future trips to the USA. My husband rented a car to make it easier for us and the meeting took around five minutes but checks before and after were very long. The man just saw a disabled person in front of him and I got a travel visa for ten years, not even one question was asked.

In the May/June (the time of my birthday), Misio and I flew to Florida for the first time ever (my BFF Phoebe was already living there). We both very much liked this adventure, as it is very accessible and hot out there. We not only spent time with Phoebe, but also explored Florida's crucial landmarks like Disneyland, Busch Gardens (with amazing rollercoasters), Space Centre, Miami and Key West to name but a few. We even saw a huge head of a real alligator in the wild (he was trying to stay in the shade, as it was a very hot day) and I got a birthday cake in the shape of a huge hamburger and a voucher to McDonald's (yes, they have such vouchers). My husband and I were laughing that some stereotypes about America and Americans are true. They even have drive through ATMs, big portions of food and you have to tip everyone (even the guy who puts your takeaway pizza in the box).

At the end of June that year my husband and I went to London to see Michael Bublè in the British Summer Time concert. It is very important to mention that with me being disabled, my husband has been responsible for making sure that I can easily access these different places and sites. It was like that this time too. After a few days in London, he took me to the airport and I flew myself to Poland to visit my family, for the first time after my brain injury.

In October, we went to the Manchester area with my husband's parents. In fact, once a year they always take us for family holidays somewhere for a week either just with them or other family members too. Misio took me for a tour around Manchester City's stadium, and Manchester City are now my team, it really helps that they have a handsome manager.

The next year, at the end of January we went to Manchester to see *Strictly Come Dancing* live, however now I know that shows to watch in the arena are simply not for me, with my current sight.

In April 2019, on Easter Saturday, we flew back to Florida for another fortnight. This time we also spent some time with Phoebe and her boyfriend (handsome, from Cuba) and visited a few landmarks like amazing rollercoasters in Busch Gardens or a crazy ride on the airboat in the Everglades. However, this adventure was more focused on relaxing than on sightseeing. This is why we decided to spend some time in Key Largo and we had a great time there, we also got serious tans.

At the end of May, my husband took me back to Manchester Arena for a Michael Bublè concert again (music concerts in the arena are good for me in my current situation). Then in the beginning of July, I flew myself to Poland to visit my family and Misio came over for a long weekend (my last weekend in Poland), on the night of our fourth wedding anniversary. For our first holidays in an adapted caravan, we went back to Wemyss Bay in Western Scotland at the end of August. My husband loved the fact that I could wash the dishes, as a sink was also adapted to my needs. In the second week of October we went on a week's holiday to Nairn with my husband's family, except his niece and nephew, who went away with the other grandparents. At the end of this trip, my husband's sister Mary-Jane and her husband Peter offered to lend us some money, as we had told the whole family earlier that we had started to save for our own house (it was actually because of some money we got from Misio's auntie and uncle which we had used to start a 'Help to Buy' ISA).

We talked it (the offer) through and decided to use their help. I then started a serious house hunt, with four general conditions in mind. We decided that our future property needed to have two bedrooms, to be a bungalow or ground floor flat, to be close to my husband's work and to be in Clackmannanshire, so I could stay with the same care provider (it would take months to get a new one). The flat we actually bought was the second property that we put an offer on. You could say that I obsessively searched for a new property and I pointed out to my husband that the second bedroom in the flat we bought was actually big enough. We both fell in love with this place and put in an offer during the viewing. It took just a month and a week before we got keys to our own home and it was Tony (Pepper's husband), who made sure that buying our first house was a very easy experience for both of us.

6
My current daily routine and my life now

I have been fully home for just over two and a half years and my daily routine has changed a lot, as I get bored very quickly and easily. I have not been at work for four and a half years now and being perfectly honest, I really miss it. I miss being needed and useful. I am confined to a wheelchair, have facial palsy on my left side and therefore my speech is not so clear and I slaver (I have already had two plastic surgeries on my left cheek and was supposed to have a meeting, when the whole pandemic kicked off). I am still not happy with the left side of my face to the extent that I simply do not look in the mirror (I still compare my look to the one before the issues with my health). Besides, my eyesight is not great. Jumpy eyes, of which one covered during the day with an eye patch (I was supposed to see my ophthalmologist but then the pandemic started). This does not help with learning how to walk again but nevertheless I am still trying and my private physiotherapist was visiting me every three weeks before the pandemic. The obstacles are not only problems with my eyesight but also a lack of balance and dexterity and the fact that I am lacking sensitivity in the right side of my whole body; it is better now but still my right arm and leg feel a little numb and weird. The level of my physical disability hinders me from working. No one expected (not even my neurologist) that the side effects of the surgery would appear all at once and totally change my life.

How do they say ‘When you get lemons, make the lemonade’ or something like that? I am trying to do it. I know that I am not able to work or actually do much because of my physical disability but I can still do things with my mind. As previously mentioned, I get bored with my daily routine, therefore I have changed it a lot over the time I have been back home. Talking about my daily routine and my life it is very hard not to mention the global pandemic, which has changed everybody's life, even mine. You could say that I was already social distancing before, but now my weekly 'adventure' has stopped. I used to make Misio take me somewhere at the weekends but it has changed because of my glasses getting steamed up when I wear a mask in public, which is mandatory in Scotland.

Lockdown has changed our lives completely (we had just managed to adapt our garden to my needs before the whole global crisis) but everyone has noticed that. Yet some people are simply very selfish in my opinion. I am thinking about those who do not social distance or wear masks or those who moan about quarantine when coming back from holidays. I have just one thing to say: "The sun will be here or there next year, but they might not be". For the love of God, there is a global pandemic! Are they really expecting to go about their lives as normal?!

Even our life together has changed considerably. My husband still works from home and it is already the second half of August. For the first nine weeks of the UK's lockdown he was my main caretaker with my normal care providers dealing with my morning visits, while he was working. In week ten of lockdown, my usual care providers started to do my social visits a few times a week. Gradually, they have reintroduced my social visits every day. From 31st August (after our holidays), my husband has already asked for visits to be reinstated as before lockdown, in preparation for his return to the office around November.

As previously mentioned, I get bored with my routine and keep changing it and it has been like this since lockdown started too. At the beginning I was watching TV in the morning and in the evening but it was just too much and therefore I have started to study Spanish to exercise and stimulate my brain more. My current daily routine has evolved around studying and exercising. I do have a lot of time on my hands and am very wary about my diet and the fact that I spend most of my time sitting. That is why I do exercise a lot (Misio even jokes that he would have a six pack, if he exercised that much). The exercises help me not only to manage my size, but also to structure my day. In January 2019, I joined the MPC programme founded by the Outlander star and have been a member ever since, although I do need to tailor the exercises to my special needs. My current daily routine is as follows:

Monday – Friday

Alarm at 8:20 a.m. and bed exercises, which include:
General cardio warmup and mobility drills (all these help me to stretch and warm my body up after the night)
Four rounds of the following five exercises, with twenty five repetitions of each one (crunches; glut raises; v sit ups; horizontal scissors; chest presses or leg curls) (depending on the day). I then do seventy five push ups from knees; twenty five superman and three x two minute push up planks from the knees.

At 9:15 a.m. my morning visit starts (for an hour)
During this time my care providers deal with my bed stretches, which I treat as my Cool Down. They also take me to the toilet, help me with my shower, put on my clothes, prepare my breakfast and coffee. Before eating and drinking I take my meds also prepared by them (I take six pills in the morning).

Around 11 a.m. my dad calls me for a daily catch up, after which I start to study Spanish.

Around 1:30 p.m. I have my lunch (at the moment my husband prepares it).

Around 2-2:30 p.m. I start my social visit with my care providers and it lasts for one and a half hours. During this visit I am entitled to do whatever but I focus on exercising to keep my weight stable at least, or to lose some. During this time my carers assist me with practising walking (three times) and squats (three x ten reps) and lunges (three x ten reps for each leg) on the parallel bars. They help me to get on and off my recumbent exercise bike, on which I cycle for thirty minutes with changing resistance. Then they put weights on my wrists (2.5 kg on each) and I do three rounds of six arm exercises with twenty five reps of each one. After all these exercises I get refreshed by my care providers, they also change my top, take me to the toilet and leave me by the kitchen table with my husband or sit me down on the couch in the living room. It really depends if I had my lunch or not before my exercises (if my social visit started at or before 2 p.m., I would have my lunch later).

After 3:30-4:00 p.m. I often finish my Spanish lesson and my mum calls me for a daily chat.

Around 6 p.m. my husband prepares the dinner for both of us, after which we usually watch the TV or I write or play on my iPad or check 'my addiction'.

Around 11 p.m. my husband gives me meds (two pills), takes me to the toilet and bed.

Saturday

My morning routine is the same, I do all my bed exercises and my carers assist me as usual. Additionally, I do all my afternoon exercises in the morning with assistance from my husband. I also do thirty minutes of yoga. In the afternoon I relax.

Sunday

It is a day of total rest from any form of exercise.

The above routine is my current routine, from week to week with visits from friends or to the in-laws at the weekends. It is worth mentioning that before the lockdown rules were softened, my husband and I were spending weekends only in each other's company, being in the touch with others only by phone or the internet.

Talking about lockdown you cannot avoid the subject of the 'Black Lives Matter' movement, which became more active after police brutality towards black people again (the killing of another black unarmed man by brutal mostly white police officers in the USA). In the time of global pandemic people (mostly black but white too) took to the streets and organised peaceful protests around the world, despite putting one another at risk of infection by taking part in mass gatherings. It must mean that they really are frustrated and angry. Misio and I watched a few documentaries and movies about police brutality and systematic racism towards people of colour, especially in the USA, but also in the UK. I want to highlight that Americans have a very important and huge test this autumn to prove that they truly do not discriminate against anyone because of their race, gender, religion or sexuality.

Being white Caucasian, born and brought up in mostly white Poland, I have started to question myself about my attitude to the whole issue of 'Black Lives Matter'. I was not aware and the fact that it is still such a huge problem in our times (this would be because of my white privilege that as white person, I have never experienced such brutality from forces who were supposed to protect me), but unfortunately this still exists. I feel powerless, that is why I decided to sign a petition to the British parliament to make it mandatory for British kids to study British history with all its 'doom and gloom' periods.

7
My loved ones

I understand that my disability has not only changed my life but also that of those around me. Being confined to a wheelchair has influenced the lives of my husband, my parents, my brother, my husband's family and my friends.

My husband has the 'wonderful opportunity' to experience that every day and all the time. My physical disability means that I require help with everything. I have care providers who deal with my morning routine six times a week and my social visits five times a week and from September they will be dealing with my lunch routine (I will be back to the pre-lockdown routine) five times a week. My husband takes care of me after he finishes his work and with lunch but only until September. At the weekends, apart from Saturday morning visits from my carers, solely my husband helps me. It needs to be said here that he is my everything, from my beautician to my personal trainer and psychologist. What is more, he deals with everything concerning the house itself and any housework on top of his job. He was my rock when I was in the hospitals and care home. He is still my rock just now when I am at home. In the days of my craziness and problems with breathing and swallowing, he was seriously struggling, although I did not know about that at the time. With time, he got used to our new life and learned to accept the big changes. I will always remember his reaction to me saying, just before I moved to the care home, that he did not sign up for this, when he married me and that he could leave. He just said that he was in the worst with me and why would he leave at that time, when things were starting to look better? He also said I did not sign up for this either. Now I totally understand the meaning of the saying that 'Good things come to those who wait' and I waited five long years for the proposal.

My family's life has been affected too. It was very hard at first for them to get used to the fact that their youngest child and younger sister had a brain haemorrhage, was hospitalised for a long time then in the care home and has ended up being confined to a wheelchair. They were waiting for grandchildren and nieces or nephews, not me being disabled. They are very supportive, although we live in different countries. I have daily chats with my parents and my brother calls me every so often to check how I am doing. Because of the global pandemic their visits here and mine to Poland have simply stopped. They had started to visit me more since I went to hospital, especially my mum. Actually, she was visiting and helping me, when I was hospitalised for the first time. There was a time she would fly back home for work and come back here for the next weekend. She learned sooner than my dad and my brother to accept my new circumstances and was there for me sooner. She did not like the times when it was really bad with me, but she decided to face the facts and be close to me no matter what.

My dad had a totally different approach, which I believe to be caused by his inability to help me, with my brother having a similar approach. My dad never wanted to talk to me about my disability when I needed to vent my thoughts and frustration about my new reality. These different approaches to their child's disability did not help my parents' marriage. My mum expected some conversation about my new life and support when she was tired of being strong for me. My dad on the other hand was struggling to make sense of these dramatic changes and would not offer such comfort. I sometimes think that they would be better off separate from each other. I know that it is quite harsh to say that but that is how I feel sometimes. It is like they have lost the ability to communicate with each other because they both see my disability from different perspectives and do not want to see it from the other one's.

My disability has changed not only my husband's life but also lives of members of his family, who visited me in the hospital, in the care home and still do so now too. They do not fuss about me but when we go on holidays together they always make sure that the accommodation suits my needs. Because of the global pandemic we have not seen them as often as before.

Because of the global pandemic we have not seen most of our friends for a long time now. They were also shocked at the changes to my health and life. They visited me in the hospitals and later in the care home. I must say that in general the girls seem to be stronger or better at pretending to keep their cool when they are faced with their friend's sickness. They are still supportive and always make sure that the places of our meet-ups are accessible for me or check on me every so often if they live outside Scotland.

8
My thoughts about my disability

It is not easy actually to live by the title. I would even argue that 'exhaling the past' is actually very hard, especially when your past was totally different from your present and what your future will be.

I know that looking back does not help but unfortunately I am still not able to forget about my past. Writing down my memories was less and less enjoyable. It was fun to write about my childhood and my teenage years, about my studies in Poland and then in Scotland and the time I met my husband and our different adventures but the closer I was getting to my new reality the harder it was to just treat it as the past. The near past where I did not think that something like this was waiting for me just behind the turn on my life's road.

It is hard to forget about plans I had then, when everything seemed possible. I imagined our new and bigger family, when I was thinking about the near future, instead I became disabled and am not able to take care even of myself. We were planning a baby just after the wedding, not hospitals, care home and a wheelchair.

I know that I need to try harder not to look back, to 'inhale the future', which for someone my age especially is difficult, when the past accounts for most of my life until I became disabled. It would not be possible to bear it without the support of my loved ones.

My husband and I want to buy a pug puppy in the near future, to go back to Florida and to Australia when it is safe to do so but for now we have two staycations to look forward to in Scotland in this crazy year.

However, I do not want to plan too far ahead, as everything might change one day and I know that very well from experience.

‘The show must go on…’

9
And another year

…and it does, although 2020 has been a very crazy and weird year for everyone everywhere. Naively, we all thought that it would just be a few months. How wrong we were. This is why most people have not planned any overseas holidays this year and we have already welcomed spring 2021. We are all hoping that staycations will be allowed at least, after lockdowns in all four parts of the United Kingdom (although the restrictions differ between parts of the UK) finish. In 2020 we (my husband and I) went on one of two staycations planned for that year a week in Grannies Heilan Hame Caravan Park. The other staycation was cancelled due to another lockdown. We were supposed to go on it with my husband's family (like every year).

The global pandemic is still in full swing, but jabs created by different pharmaceutical giants cooperating with famous schools and some governments give hope that we can see the light at the end of the tunnel and will win the fight with this virus. Being confined to a wheelchair gave me a priority and I have already been given the first jab. Second night after it was quite difficult for me but it finished by next morning. My husband had his first one around three weeks after me, as he was qualified for it as an unpaid carer.

In the beginning of the year I had a little health scare. After two courses of antibiotics from GPs, a visit to a specialist and a little procedure the problem has been resolved and all is good now. However, I am still confined to a wheelchair with facial palsy, therefore it is hard to understand me and of course my jumpy eyes. Nothing has changed, I still require help with everything. Actually, one thing has changed – I do not wear an eyepatch anymore.

I still get easily bored so I have been writing, reading, surfing the internet and bingeing series on Netflix in order to kill my boredom between visits from my caregivers and to exercise my brain. Also, last September in 2020 and again in this past February, I have done a sponsored cycle of 12 km a day for twenty seven and twenty four days respectively, on my recumbent exercise bike in support of two UK charities. I still exercise a lot (I have just started my third year of MPC) to kill the time, structure my day but mostly to keep my weight under control.

Although we are now in another lockdown (to be perfectly honest, I have lost count), it feels to me like it has been constant since last March in 2020. Since the beginning of this time I have not seen my family in person. Thanks to apps like WhatsApp and FaceTime, we are able to see one another but it is not the same, obviously. Because of the global pandemic, I have not had a chance to take part in my granny's funeral or support my cousins after the sudden death of my mum's younger sister. Fortunately, good news came too. One of my cousins has gotten engaged, and so have Rachel and Phoebe.

My husband is still my rock and my 'Jack of all trades' from my beautician to my psychologist. On top of that he still solely runs our house and is my caregiver in the evenings and at the weekends. It has been almost a year since he started to work from home due to the global pandemic. I must admit that I do like having him home. He is working in the other room but I feel better knowing that I am not alone. What is more, we both are aware of the fact that he is extremely lucky to have a job in the current global situation. To add to all of that, we own a small pug dog and my husband is his main caretaker, which includes taking him for walks, feeding, playing, grooming and cleaning up after him, to name just a few. I really feel for my husband. I totally understand that it must be very hard, when you have so much on your plate and I really wish I could make it easier for him.

The pug is called 'Toadie' after the small ogre from *Gummi Bears*. He was almost eight weeks when we got him at the very end of October 2020 and he is almost seven months now. He has grown a lot, from such a small puppy, looking like a cuddly toy at first. The friendship and respect between Toadie and my husband are just priceless. I could scream and scream and Toadie does not listen, but a simple "no" from my husband and he obeys. Toadie is a great companion for both us and a little ray of sunshine in these dark times.

It is very hard to plan anything nowadays. Not only my fear of the possibility that plans may have to drastically change overnight but all these lockdowns, quarantine rules, social distancing and face masks influence our plans. Hoping that staycations will be allowed, as we are going to Wemyss Bay Caravan Park for a week in the beginning of June. Maybe another staycation with my husband's family in October and I would like to visit my family in Poland, but those are the only plans for this year.

‘Do not judge a book by its cover’
My disabled life

Contents:

1

Determination

I have always been very determined. I have made a choice to live my life to the fullest, despite the fact that my new life is very unexpected and very different to the one I had before. Understandably, it was a very big shock to me and my loved ones in the beginning. In fact, it took a me good few years and long periods of time spent away from home to learn to accept my new reality – being confined to a wheelchair.

I eventually came back home and decided that I had to fight for myself and my husband. I knew that I was too young to give up, although my life was completely different to how my husband and I had planned.

I eventually started my council physio meetings once a week, which lasted for a year (twice as long as they were expecting), but I knew that it was not enough. Despite the fact that my strength and coordination were better, the ultimate goal was not achieved – I was still unable to walk. It was suggested that I should join a club for disabled people but I decided eventually against it. Having lots of human interaction on a daily basis and being disabled only physically not mentally, I became more determined to regain my physical strength and ability to walk again in my own home. My husband and I decided to buy parallel bars to practice my walking and a recumbent exercise bike to do some cardio and we turned our spare bedroom into my own gym. With help from carers I am able to do my exercises daily.

Daily exercises and watching what I eat have not only structured my day but also have helped me to stay in control of my weight. I have become very determined about keeping my weight the same, if not losing some of it. I have even added some additional exercises suggested by my private physio, on top of interval cycling and squats in the parallel bars. I have started to do back split squats for each leg. Unfortunately, due to the global pandemic my private physio's visits were terminated, however this has not stopped me. On the contrary, I became more determined to use this period of time to my advantage. I knew that it was only me that could help with my own rehabilitation and weight control by actually exercising daily with my carers or my husband. My carers get very tired just by watching me, at least that is what they say and they always admire my determination and resilience in keeping doing it, despite the daunting reality.

You could even say that I became more determined in my daily life. I seem to invest myself fully in whatever I am doing, which works even when I feel down. Do not get me wrong, I do have days when I feel demotivated and I am questioning my exercise regime but then if I do not exercise, I feel really bad. At times, I feel very frustrated that it takes so much of my effort to control my weight, taking into account my lack of movement and some other medical issues (underactive thyroid).

I am determined that I will walk again one day. It has been a good few years since I became disabled though. Even so, I truly hope that maybe medical development will be able to help me to do that sometime in the near future.

2
Identity

I have been living in Scotland since September 2006. My identity has always been a little problematic, since settling down in Scotland especially. This September I will be celebrating fifteen years here and it was supposed to be just for one year, as previously mentioned. I have spent most of my adult life in Scotland. I have grown older here and I have gotten used to the Scottish way of life, which is totally different than the Polish one. I notice this any time I visit my family and friends there. The identity as far as my nationality and country of residence are concerned has always been a bit problematic for me. I was born and raised in Poland but I have spent my adulthood mostly in Scotland. You could say that I am Polish at my core but I have been shaped as a relatively young adult here in Scotland. Having spent just few years here, I have already formed an opinion that people like me should not have a right to decide about any of aspect of the lives of people living in Poland. I must admit that this opinion only got stronger over the years that I have spent here in Scotland.

Unfortunately, my application for British citizenship has failed and I have only Settled Status. This is why I do not feel like I belong to any country. The application was filled in earlier (when I still could walk but not commute) but submitted almost a year later (when I had already been in the care home). The local MP's signature and query with parliamentary ombudsman even on top of my lengthy explanations about possible mistakes deriving from the fact that I became disabled in the meantime, have not influenced any change and my application has been rejected. It has been a very costly endeavour in the monetary sense and a very time consuming one.

Now that I am disabled my identity issues are even more complicated. When a person meets me for the first time, they see a girl in a wheelchair and remember me, as Magda in a wheelchair and my identity concerning my country of origin fades away. I suppose, any wheelchair is very distinctive when describing its user. My 'trademark' used to be my accent but now it is my wheelchair. My wheelchair defines me, whether I like it or not and most of the time I do not. Seeing a wheelchair, most people will think that I am mentally disabled, as well. Being perfectly honest, I am really fed up with being spoken to like I do not understand or know things. I totally understand that it is very hard to understand my speech (as previously mentioned, I have a facial palsy on the left side of my face) and prefer therefore when a person tells me directly that they do not get what I am saying instead of pretending that they do understand me. My blurry speech really does not make it easy to communicate and the perception of me as a disabled person, but only physically.

What is more, I am able to identify myself as a very supported daughter and younger sister, loved wife but I will never be able to identify myself as a mother in a real sense of that word. Being mummy to Toadie is not the same, obviously.

3

Survivor

Since my brain bleed and becoming confined to a wheelchair, I always wanted a tattoo when I came back home fully. I have the word SURVIVOR tattooed on my right forearm, as a reminder that I have survived a brain injury.

Obviously, I am very glad that I am a survivor. I am very grateful that this nightmare (my constantly declining health) has been done and dusted. I must admit that it was very close to the end on two occasions. The first time was when my bleed happened and I was told by one of the doctors that I had been 'lucky' that it had been outside and not inside my brain. The second time was when I had problems with breathing and swallowing and my husband and my mum were informed that it could go either way with me. However, '*I am still standing*', like the song by Elton John, to be precise it should be more like I am still sitting, or like the song by Destiny's child, *I'm a survivor*.

What is more, I am very grateful to all the staff from different hospitals, the care home and my home carers for their help and all the care given before or being given to me on a daily basis. This is why I have decided to give a little back in a way possible to me, by doing two sponsored cycles on my recumbent exercise bike in support of two UK charities, as previously mentioned.

To be perfectly honest, I have darker thoughts sometimes. Do not get me wrong here, I am not brave enough, besides my thoughts are not so dark. Sometimes, I just think that my loved ones, my husband especially, would be much better off without me. I am sure that his life would be much easier, taking into consideration that I need constant help with everything and my walking abilities do not seem to improve with time.

4

Ability

It is very hard to stop myself from comparing my new reality with my previous life when I was fully able to take good care of myself and others, when only the sky was my limit, when I could do anything, anytime, anywhere and with anyone. I think that it is so hard for me because I became disabled relatively early in my adult life.

Being disabled and confined to a wheelchair mean rthat I have lost all of my independence. I need help literally with everything, even when I have to use the bathroom. I must admit that it is very hard for me (feels almost shameful and embarrassing) to ask my husband or my carers for anything but I also understand that I am not able to do anything without their help.

The level of my disability prevents me from working or doing anything physical, like even running a house. The simplest task takes me ages and requires help from others. It is very hard to forget about my job. Not the act of working itself but the fact of using my brain and of feeling useful and needed. I am lacking that now, that is why I am trying to fill the void of not working, which was very stimulating for my brain, by different morning activities.

I am very unhappy when I am not able to finish a task, therefore I simply do not do it at all. I feel very useless, very dependent and needy, like I am some kind of obstacle or piece of furniture. In order to do something and fill out my day, I spend time exercising.

I do not like it when others tell me how amazing I am doing not giving up. I am sure that they would do the same in my shoes. I did not plan to be disabled, but it has happened and I have to use the abilities which I have left, which are mostly mental ones.

5

Beauty

I have never had high self-esteem but now it is even lower. I always was a chubby kid, then the biggest girl in my group of friends and admirers also showed up much later. I have never been a 'beauty' who everyone has been admiring. There is a Polish saying that every 'monster' will find its admirer eventually and so I did too. I have now been married for almost six years.

I became disabled after marrying my husband and thanks to God for that, as even I would not marry myself looking like I do just now. During my move from a rehab hospital to a care home, my husband turned out to be a true man. He had made his decision to stay by my side no matter what, when I said that he was free to go as he had not signed up for this when he had married me. Now, I am also grateful for the lengthy relationship before the engagement. I had managed to dazzle him enough to stay with me no matter what my outside beauty, which is very questionable now.

I am not only confined to a wheelchair but also I have a facial palsy on the left side of my face therefore my speech is not great and I have jumpy eyes, as previously explained. What can I say, simply Miss World! This is why you can only see one of my fingers on any picture taken after I became disabled to prove that I have been in different places too. For the same reason, there is only one small mirror in our home. I not only do not like to see myself now but also hear myself, as I compare how I looked and sounded before. I really do not know how both my husband and mum are able to understand me without repeating myself too much.

I have mentioned already that I decided to take control of my weight, keep it stable at least. It is very easy for me to put it on, but very hard to lose it, because I just sit constantly, additionally my thyroid is underactive. In order to do that – to fight the kilograms – I exercise a lot and watch what I eat, which is very hard, taking into consideration that I have a sweet tooth and simply love chocolate.

6

Life

My daily routine has not changed that much, although it has stabilized. My home carers care for me until 4 p.m. and after his work my husband takes over. I wake up every weekday morning with my alarm and do my bed exercises. Then, my home carers come to help me with my morning routine and after 10:45 I start my day. Then, my dad calls me for a daily chat and after that I check my social media accounts and my email or I spend this time watching Netflix or Amazon Prime Video but sometimes I just shop or write a book or read something on my kindle. As previously mentioned, I get bored easily and therefore change my morning activities quite often but at the same time I get easily addicted to them. This means that I will be focused on one activity all the time until it is finished.

My lunch visit starts at 13:30 and is followed by a social visit, during which I do my exercises in the parallel bars, ride my exercise bike and exercise my arms using weights. After all that exercise, my carers refresh me and take me to the toilet. Then my mum calls for a daily chat. When my husband finishes his work, he solely cares for me till the next morning. In the evenings, we both watch TV or I am dealing with the activity that I have been addicted to at the time. This happens from Monday through to Friday. Weekends are different as my husband does not work, but same as previously mentioned, I do all my afternoon exercises in the morning, so the second half of Saturday and Sunday (total rest day, same as before) I can devote to spending time with my husband and Toadie. Before the global pandemic, we would go to visit someone or host them or simply go shopping. I know that is weird but when I am only with my husband it feels less daunting. The fact that my carers appear after a weekend, being disabled feels more real.

Thanks to technology, we have managed to meet our friends virtually on a few occasions. There is also a chance that we can see some of them living here in Scotland in person, as lockdown rules have been eased a little. I am also using it to video call my family, who I have not seen live for quite some time now.

It is very nice to meet friends and their families. On the other hand, meeting them can be quite hard. I feel that the life of my husband and I has stopped and changed so much that it will never be like theirs.

Though, *Life is life (na na na na nah)…*

7

Emotions

Being disabled brings many emotions up for me. At first, I was very angry, confused and surprised, I could not believe that it was happening to me. I felt lost, powerless and very sad. I was not able to see my future and that scared me a lot. I was crying a lot and all that energy had been wasted instead of helping my rehab.

Then, I just wanted not to be afraid to drink and swallow. I have just been very tired of my constantly declining health. In the care home, I was more accepting of my new reality and I was getting stronger and less dependent on around the clock care. After fully coming back home, I have started to get stronger, more determined and accepting. I have kept changing my routine, as previously mentioned. I get easily bored too, therefore I keep choosing different activities to fill my mornings, which I have already explained.

Being disabled brings up very contrasting emotions too. On one hand, I want to be treated like a fully functional adult but I also expect and want help, as I know that I am not able to do things by myself.

Do not get me wrong, I do have good and bad days. When it is a good day, I am more determined and optimistic. I also look forward more to my exercises and I seem to be more accepting of my new reality. I simply seem to get on with my disabled life. On the bad days, I am more sad and angry with my new reality. I dwell more on my past, compare myself to the young woman I was before and bring up all the things out of my reach now. My poor husband just sighs when I start to complain again.

8

Devotion

I really won a lucky ticket on the life lottery when I married my husband almost six years ago. A lengthy relationship before getting engaged and marriage has turned out to be my blessing. He has been by my side from the beginning, although he thought that I had simply been a hypochondriac when they decided to leave me overnight in hospital with suspected nerve damage in my neck and it turned out to be a brain bleed.

He was and still is my rock and my everything, even more just now. He pushes me to do more or cuddles me, depending on my mood. I do not feel alone, he always has my back. His devotion to me, my disability and our little family is pure and absolute. He has made a decision to stay with me through mostly bad times. He is my shoulder to cry on on my bad days, it is also him who tries to cheer me up when I get sad.

Do not get me wrong, we do shout at each other and quarrel from time to time. Which married couple does not have different opinions sometimes? Being disabled does not change the fact that I am still his wife.

If you enjoyed 'Exhale the past, inhale the future' keep reading for the short story 'Never too late'.

Never too late

Magdalena Stewart

1

Molly was so much into the book she was reading that she did not notice who sat next to her when the tube has stopped in one of its stations. To be perfectly honest, she did not care because she was in her imaginary world of hopeless romance through the characters of the book she was reading. She was imagining that she was that girl in the book.

In reality she was a single chick with a huge appetite for romance straight from American rom-coms. She was about to turn thirty and start her brand-new job in one of London's finest lifestyle magazines as an assistant to one of the executive editors. She had decided that it was high time to take some risks in her life. She had left her small hometown and her very organised and predictable life to try something new. She wanted to be more anonymous, she wanted her life to just happen and not to be judged by her neighbours or some random people like it was in her hometown. She was also a hopeless romantic and hoped to meet the love of her life and to be swept off her feet like the female characters in the books she simply adored.

Suddenly, all the lights in the whole tube train went off and it got very dark, pitch black you could say. Molly screamed a little and jumped a little on her seat. She also grabbed the person next to her. She was not entirely sure what she grabbed as it was so dark but it felt like someone's knee. Molly was petrified of the darkness so she grabbed the knee even harder. She had always been terrified of the dark, for as long as she could remember.

It felt like an eternity for her but it had really been just a few moments in fact. Long enough though to leave her a little bit anxious and uneasy. Suddenly a male voice asked: "Are you ok?"

Molly turned her head to the side of the voice and she literally froze on the spot. She was not able to speak, which was not usual for her. She opened her eyes even wider. She was looking at her ideal man, who could easily be a character from her books. Her heart started to beat a little faster but she knew it was insane and she was little bit flustered but she managed to respond eventually:

"I am …I am very sorry for grabbing you …I meant your knee!"

"No worries! " He smiled at her and asked again, "Are you ok?"

"I am fine, thank you! The thing is that I am very scared of the darkness and was a little bit panicked when the lights went off. I am very sorry ... " Molly explained quietly.

"It is fine. Not every day your knee gets squeezed like that!" He laughed quietly but then he added, "It really is ok! Do not worry about it!" when he noticed Molly was embarrassed. Then, he suddenly asked "What are you reading? It must be very interesting as you were very engrossed in your book when the lights went off!"

"It is nothing interesting, just some girly stuff!" responded a flustered Molly.

How to say to the man of your dreams that you like romantic cliches and dream about a feeling like that, it was rather embarrassing. She simply did not know what else to say but it was her tube stop and she took a deep breath and said: "I am very sorry but the next tube stop is mine."

"Sure, no problem! Have a good afternoon! Do not grab others like that!" He laughed quietly...

Molly took off from the tube as it was her stop. *Thank God!* she thought to herself. *It would be rather embarrassing if he knew what I was reading!* She was thinking about her mystery guy from the tube. She was even analyzing his last words to her. *Would he be jealous or did it really hurt him and he just wanted to spare others the pain?* She could not stop thinking about him. *Those eyes when I gazed at him. His tone of voice ...Ok, stop it Molly! He was just nice to you! That is it!*

She did know it was just a normal interaction but she could not stop herself from re-living it and imagine herself in his strong arms. Her journey home from the tube station seemed very short though.

Molly saw the mystery guy in the tube on numerous occasions. They even exchanged smiles and gazed in a friendly way at each other. However, they never shared any more close encounters.

Molly was not aware that she would get to know her mystery guy from the tube one day.

2

Luke got up quite early on this Saturday morning and he was just about to take a shower when his mobile phone rang. It was his granny, Jenny, so he picked up.

"Hello Granny!" said Luke.

"Hi Luke! I am very sorry for calling you so early but I have a bit of an emergency, " said Jenny.

"Are you ok?" asked Luke immediately.

"Yeah! Do not worry, I am fine! I just have a huge favour to ask. Would it be possible for you to come over to mine and I will explain thoroughly what favour I need from you? I will make your favourite breakfast! Pancakes with fresh blueberries, strawberries and whipped cream!"

"You know how to encourage me, Granny! I'll just take a quick shower and the tube then! I should not be longer than an hour or so," said Luke enthusiastically.

As promised, Luke showed up at his granny's within an hour. She also kept her word and a delicious breakfast was served on his arrival. They started to talk straight away.

"So what is your emergency Granny?" asked Luke curiously.

"Well …first of all, I would like to apologise for calling you so early and probably waking you up! I would not call you so early but time is of the essence. You know your Auntie Jennifer is pregnant and just about to give birth, like next week?"

"Yeah?"

"She called early this morning and has asked me to come to Australia and help her with her newborn child as soon as I can. Naturally, I could not say no. I have booked my flight for tomorrow morning and I will be there twenty four hours later."

"Wow! Tomorrow?"

"Yeah! I know that it is crazy but when another grandchild is on the way and his or her mummy needs me! That is where I need you Luke!"

"You want me to go with you to Australia?" asked Luke.

"No! Not that! I need you to stay here at my flat! You see …I have this girl Molly, who is renting the flat next door and I need you to help her with any issues she may encounter while I am gone because I promised her that she could come to me with any problems with the flat. I have tried to speak to her but I have not had any luck yet but I am going to keep trying to chat with her. However, I may not manage to do this so she might be a bit surprised and confused when she learns that I have already left for Australia! What do you think, Luke?"

"Well …to be perfectly honest, it is a bit of a crazy and rushed idea but I totally understand that you want to be close to your daughter, as she really needs you just now. Having said that I would do anything for you, Granny! So if you want and need me to move in here for a bit I will do that. How long are you going to be there?"

"To be honest …I really do not know. Two or three months, I think but I am really not sure!"

"Oh, I see."

"There is something else …there is this wedding in a few weeks. I am very close with this couple and their son is getting married and I have been invited. I have already confirmed that I would attend but I will not able to as I will be in Australia. Would you be so kind and attend this wedding instead of me?"

"Sure, Granny!"

"Great …I will leave you a note with all the details and a present of course!"

"No problem, Granny!"

"You are a star, Luke! Thank you very much."

"Always, Granny! You just need to ask!"

Luke finished his favourite breakfast and decided to get back to his flat to get packed and ready for his new adventure in Jenny's flat. He also knew that he needed to speak to his flatmate and very close friend Simon.

It took him around forty minutes and he got back home. Fortunately, Simon was in and they both had a good chat. Luke explained the whole situation to Simon and advised how long it might be before he would be back. Simon was shocked a bit but knew that Luke would do it no matter what and decided not to complicate things further for his friend but to offer him his full support.

Luke decided to take with him not only some clothes and cosmetics but also his DJ's decks so he could continue with his hobby during his stay in his granny's home.

He got back to Jenny's flat that evening, before her early morning flight to Australia the next day.

3

It was the same Sunday, but late morning, when Molly decided to take a shower. Suddenly, the water turned icy cold. She screamed a little and jumped out the shower.

Luke got up very early that Sunday to see his granny before her flight to Australia. He was actually ready, showered, dressed and had had breakfast, when he heard loud knocking at an external door.

Molly checked everything and it turned out that the fault must be with her boiler. She remembered Jenny saying that she could come to her with any problem concerning the flat. Molly knew that it was one of these situations and not thinking too long she decided to use Jenny's helping hand. Jenny was her landlord and was living in the flat next door. Molly did not put in a lot of thought, wrapped herself in a bath towel and ran to Jenny's flat. She knocked loudly three times. A door opened and Molly froze on the spot.

"Hello, I am Luke, Jenny's grandson, you must be Molly," said the guy who opened the door.

"Yes, I am Molly. Could I please speak to Jenny?"

"It is rather impossible. Granny is now on the way to visit my Auntie Jennifer in Australia."

"She did not tell me that she was going away! How long will she be there? What should I do when I have a problem with the flat I am renting from her?" asked a confused Molly.

"It was just a spur of the moment decision. Auntie Jennifer, Jenny's youngest child, is expecting her second child and decided suddenly that she would like her mother to be with her. So, granny Jenny went. She did not know for sure how long she would stay there, but she reckoned two or three months at least."

"That is brilliant!" Molly said sarcastically.

"Granny left all her affairs to me in her absence. I have now moved in here and I will be your landlord for the time being. So, it is me who you can ask for help if there is any problem with the flat you are renting from her."

"I do not normally look like this. My boiler …I was having a shower and suddenly the water turned icy cold! I have checked everything and it seems that there is something wrong with the boiler."

"Can I please check this myself before calling the gas and electricity company?"

"Yeah, sure! Come on in!"

"Thanks!"

Luke checked everything and Molly was right, it was an issue with the boiler which had caused the water to turn cold. He said that he would call the company and he would keep her posted and that Molly should be patient as it was Sunday after all. He also added:

"It is not ideal but you can use Jenny's shower in the meantime. Also, I really like what you have done with this flat. It is very cosy and homely!"

"Thanks!" Molly managed to say before Luke closed the door after himself.

Thank God, thought Molly, *Thank God, I have already managed to finish my shower.*

Granny mentioned that she was younger than me but she never mentioned that she was so pretty thought Luke, leaving Molly's flat. *Come on Luke, she is way out of your league!* he said to himself when her door was closed and added in the close *But it makes the stay at Granny's far more interesting*.

4

It was Molly's first day in her new job. She felt excited but also anxious. She wanted to make a good first impression. She came into the office, which was very modern, although the building it was situated in was old and in the heart of Regent Street near Piccadilly Circus. Molly was positively surprised that the office was open plan. Molly took a deep breath and started to introduce herself to some people. It was not the end of the surprises today. The biggest one was just heading in her direction.

Molly spotted a very good-looking guy. He was tall and extremely handsome. He was simply the man of her dreams. Her knees went soft, she started to feel butterflies in her stomach but she was trying very hard not to show anything. This handsome stranger was really approaching her direction and he smiled at her.

"Hi, I am Ashley, your new boss," said the handsome man and took his right arm out to greet her hand, while continuing to speak: "You must be Molly! Very nice to finally meet you."

"Yes …yes, I am Molly. Nice to meet you too Ashley!" said Molly and shook his hand.

Ashley detected the confusion in the tone of Molly's voice and added, "You are not the first one to get confused when I introduce myself!" Suddenly he said, "Excuse me just for a moment," and went back to his office.

Molly felt really bad and embarrassed by the whole situation with Ashley. She'd assumed that her new boss would be a woman. That is why she was not able to hide her surprise when he introduced himself as her new boss. What was even worse, he was handsome and she'd got flustered about it too.

Suddenly, Molly heard a male voice behind. She turned round.

"Excuse me?" said Molly and she saw a man with a big and friendly smile.

"I was just saying that you should not worry at all! At first, I also thought that Ashley was my female boss!" said the friendly man and added, "I am Sam, nice to meet you, Molly."

"Very nice to meet you too, Sam," responded Molly.

Molly and Sam started to talk and they exchanged their different experiences about the first day in the new job. Molly learned a bit about office politics and desirable behaviour. A few moments later, Ashley came back from his office and said:

"I am very sorry Molly for disappearing on you but I had to make an urgent call in order to meet our deadline for publication."

"No problem at all! You are the boss after all!" said Molly, flustered again.

"I will get someone to show you around the office but if you have any questions and I really mean any, do not hesitate to see me …over there is my office."

He turned around and pointed to the wall behind all the desks in the back of the open plan office and added, "Where you can see this plant!"

He turned back and pointed at a desk and said,

"This is your desk, Molly. Enjoy!"

"Thank you very much, Ashley"

He then went closer to Sam and asked him to take Molly on a tour around the office in order for her to get to know the place and not to feel so alienated. After a wee chat with Sam, Ashley went back to his office. He eventually had a moment to think about his new assistant. He felt good vibes from their first encounter and hoped to get to know her better one day.

Sam was actually very happy to take Molly on the tour because he instantly felt good vibes from her. Her receptive nature, similar sense of humour and openness and eagerness to listen and learn gave Sam a feeling that they would be very close one day. Molly had a similar feeling when Sam was showing her the office and the different facilities.

Her desk was not very close to Sam's however. They were close enough though so that they could see each other due to the open plan office.

5

Molly adapted quite quickly to her new job. She even managed to convince her colleague Emily that she was not hunting for her position. Emily decided that she didn't like Molly, even before she managed to get to know her. Molly decided to give it a shot to let Emily know her better, especially because of the fact that they were sitting very close to each other and Molly did not want to make any enemies in her first week of the new job. Sam warned her about Emily. He explained to Molly that Emily had been like that with others too, at the beginning, even with him. He also advised that Molly should not worry too much about it.

It was not only at her job where Molly encountered some obstacles at first. That issue with the boiler was eventually sorted. She took up Luke's offer and had quite a few showers in Jenny's flat, which was not ideal but the only option for Molly. It also gave her an opportunity to keep a close eye on the whole repair of the boiler, as she kept harassing Luke about it. It took a few days to fix the hot water in the shower and she thought the problems had disappeared. How wrong she was.

The problem with the boiler was fixed but the washing machine broke just two days later. She thought, *This means that I have to go to Jenny's flat and inform Luke about another problem to be fixed. He will think that I am very needy!*

She left the flat in a hurry and banged on his door few times and yelled eventually,

"Luke, Luke it is Molly!"

At that time Luke was taking a shower. Through pouring water, he could hear banging on his door and Molly shouting something. He stopped the shower suddenly, wrapped a towel around his waist and answered the door with a still wet chest after few moments.

"Hi Molly! It'd better be something important because I was just having a shower, when you started to bang on my door!" said Luke calmly.

She opened her mouth wide, and when she saw him half-naked she completely forgot why she was banging on his door. It took her a minute or two to compose herself and remember why she'd gone there in the first place.

"Oh yes …my washing machine stopped working!" explained Molly eventually.

"What? Your washing machine broke? Maybe you are just pretending that the washing machine is broken so you would have a reason to see me?" joked Luke hoping that it was true

"Or maybe it is really broken!" said Molly with a hint of anger.

"Molly, calm down! That was just a stupid joke! I will come to yours. Give me five or ten minutes please."

"Thanks," said Molly.

Molly went back to her flat. She was very angry with herself for her previous outburst of anger during her conversation with Luke. However, she was trying to hide the fact that she'd totally lost her mind when she'd seen him half-naked.

As promised, Luke showed up in ten minutes, this time fully dressed. He asked to be taken to the problematic washing machine. He also thought to himself, *Man … she is very pretty*!

"It is in the kitchen," Molly said as she followed him there.

As they got in the kitchen, Luke suddenly said,

"Molly, I am very sorry for making a joke earlier. I did not think that it would make you that angry. Very sorry again!"

He felt really bad for making that joke before and did not want his new neighbour to feel uneasy and uncomfortable. Above all, Luke was genuinely afraid that Molly would find him rude, slightly sleazy and too straightforward and the truth was that he'd just started to like her that way.

"It is totally fine!" said Molly.

"I promise to be on better behaviour from now on," promised Luke.

"No problem at all, Luke," replied Molly.

Luke had checked everything and it turned out that the washing machines was indeed broken like Molly had advised earlier. He said that he would contact a specialist to check it out first. What is more, he added that he would buy a new one if it turned out that the old machine could not be fixed. He also pointed out that unfortunately it was the weekend again and therefore it might be difficult to have someone check it urgently. He said as well that Molly was most welcome to use the washing machine in his flat. He even admitted this would be inconvenient for her but necessary for the time being. Molly thanked him for the offer and explained that she would not take him up on this because she had already done her washing.

Luke left and Molly took deep breaths and thought to herself: *Thank God he did not notice that I was not angry with him, on the contrary, I was under the influence of his gorgeous physique. I was not angry with him but with myself for being speechless after seeing him shirtless.*

She also thought to herself that even the fact she seemed to like him did not change the fact that he was way out her league according to herself.

She actually took him up on his offer and used his washing machine on a few occasions. She also noticed some DJ's decks, which left her not only very curious but also proved to be very useful in the future.

6

It was Saturday afternoon when Molly heard banging on her front door. It was quite loud and sounded like someone knocking was in distress.

"Just a moment! I am coming!" said Molly loudly and she went to open the door.

She opened her door and her eyes even wider because she could not believe who she saw.

"Hi Molly!"

"Hi Sam! What are you doing here? Where is Mark?" asked a confused Molly.

"Can I come in please?" asked Sam.

"Sure! Where are my manners? Come on in!" replied Molly and let him in to her flat.

They both were in her flat and the door was locked, when Sam started to speak.

"Mark and I had a huge fight and I simply left. I am very sorry but I decided to come to you because you are just great! You listen without judging!"

"Gee, thanks! That is very nice to hear. However, I am still very confused why you are here. Do not get me wrong, I love to have you here but is it not your anniversary this weekend?" Molly asked.

"Yes!" said Sam sadly.

"So, what are you doing here at mine?"

"Well …like I said Mark and I had this huge fight and I left!"

"Yes, you have said already…but I want to know what has happened? What was the reason for your fight? Let us sit, have something to drink and talk about it!" She directed Sam to her comfy couch and asked, "First things first …what would you like to drink? I can offer you tea, coffee, water or some orange juice?"

"Coffee is fine, thank you."

It took Molly a few minutes to prepare the hot beverages for both of them, just the way they both drank their coffee in the office.

“Tell me everything! What was the reason behind your fight?” started Molly, just after she sat down next to Sam.

“Well …we started to quarrel about nothing really … napkins …it was nothing but I got really angry, I lost my temper and I said things that I really regret now,” said Sam. He was very sad and almost cried.

“I see. Was there any reason behind you being angry? Did Mark do or say anything earlier that made you lose your temper? Did anyone else say or do anything that made you angry beforehand?”

“Actually, yes. My mum called before our fight with her usual chat!” admitted Sam

“Did her call make you angry?” Molly asked.

“Yes …actually, very! She does not get it. It is not just a phase. I really love Mark and I cannot imagine my life without him. She cannot or does not want to understand that this is me. That I am who I am!”

“It sounds to me that you were angry before your fight with Mark,” said Molly after few moments and added: “Have you told Mark about your telephone conversation with your mother?”

“No, I have not!” replied Sam.

“I think that conversation made you lose your temper before your fight with Mark! Did you not tell me some time ago that Mark had had a similar problem with his parents before?” Molly asked.

“That is correct! He actually has had very similar issues with his parents. Do you think that I should have mentioned this to him?” Sam asked.

“Sure! Who would better understand you than him? Just saying!”

“Oh Molly! I should have told him, shouldn’t I?” asked Sam with noticeable worry in his voice.

"Do not worry, Sam! I am sure that Mark will understand your behaviour when you explain to him exactly why you lost your temper before your fight!"

"Yeah, at least it would explain why I behaved like I did!"

"Exactly! You really should speak to Mark and explain about your conversation with your mother and its influence on your mood."

"Thank you, Molly," said Sam, more optimistically.

"For what?" Molly asked, surprised.

"For listening! For not judging! For helping me realize the root cause of me losing my temper during my fight with Mark!" explained Sam.

"Not a problem! Always happy to listen!" Molly said with a big smile.

"I think that now is the time to speak to Mark."

"I think that too! After all it is still the weekend of your anniversary!" said Molly, smiling at Sam.

Sam left promptly, promising Molly to let her know soon how it went with Mark.

Two hours later Molly received a text message from Sam saying that they had talked about the fight and Sam's conversation with his mother. The message also confirmed Molly's assumption that Mark would understand the struggle that Sam was facing.

After this weekend Sam thanked her again and said that he and Mark would like to invite her for drinks sometime suitable for her as a token of gratitude for her help with their fight and an opportunity for Mark to finally meet Molly.

7

It was the middle of the week and nothing was really pointing out that this would be a very different day from Molly's normal weekdays. After all she was already familiar with the politics in her office and nothing could surprise her, or so she thought …

She came to the office a little bit earlier as usual and found a note on her desk. *Please come to see me.* It was signed by Ashley. He wanted to get to know her on a personal level and the opportunity presented itself on that day.

Molly was really nervous as it sounded very serious. She was very relieved when he explained to her that it was not anything wrong, quite the opposite actually. That day Molly was to assist him with some business meetings concerning the magazine that they were both working for. Ashley mentioned that he would need her a whole day therefore they would grab some lunch between the planned meetings, on the magazine's account of course. Molly was a bit shocked that it was her who had been chosen but also very excited.

The morning went very fast and it was time for lunch. "Anywhere!" responded Molly, when Ashley asked her where she would like to have lunch. He suggested that they should have it in the Canary Wharf where they were and had their first meeting after lunch. They stayed there to cut the time on traveling.

Ashley got them quite a good table with a very comfortable booth. They had ordered and were waiting for their food and drinks.

Molly did not know how but the conversation had changed from lighthearted to more serious. They both had a feeling that they could share their deepest thoughts with each other.

"So, Molly, why London?" asked Ashley. "I am asking Molly and not my subordinate!"

"Well …I wanted a change, I wanted to be more anonymous, I was kind of suffocating …no one was expecting my decision to leave my perfect and well - organised life …even my boyfriend …who loved himself, his job and then me …I was in third place. Everything was planned for me and if I stayed my life would be perfect …but only from a distance …I had to challenge myself and learn from my own mistakes and that is why I chose London. And you Ashley, are you from here?"

"Well …yes and no. I was born and grew up here then I met my wife and moved away from London with her."

"Sorry, I did not know that you have a wife!" said Molly, surprised.

"To be perfectly honest, no one at work knows …apart from you now. We have been separated for almost one year now. This has happened a few months before I took on the job as one of the executive editors here. I always wanted my personal life to stay private. Because I do not want my life's choices to be judged and people to think that they know my situation and approve or disapprove of decisions made by me. At the end of the day, it is my life!"

"Exactly! I totally agree with you, Ashley! I hated that in my life before London."

"This is why no one knows about my private life …I do not want to be judged and I do not want any pity or understanding because I know that I really damaged my marriage and I have to rebuild it and I can only do that by myself. I really love my wife and our two sons. My dad passed away when I was very young and I do not want my boys to grow up without a father too. This is why any free from work time I spend with them, trying to rebuild my wife's trust too."

"I am very sorry to hear about your dad and your problems with your marriage. To be perfectly honest, I would not expect you to have such troubles."

"Exactly! Please tell me honestly what you thought when you saw me for the first time. Do not worry, I am just trying to prove my point!"

"Well …I thought that you were very handsome, totally out my league!" said a rather embarrassed Molly. "My opinion was that you must have an easier life because of your physique, that you could have every woman and therefore you must be a womaniser."

"Gee, thanks! I really feel good about myself! I am only joking! Your first impression of me just proves my point that being regarded as handsome, guys are never taken seriously in the relationship between a man and a woman. Being regarded as handsome is a kind of curse too …"

"So, like many women would want to cheat with you but would not like to be cheated on by you!" Molly politely interrupted Ashley in order to show him that she understood his point.

"Exactly! And believe me when I say that the temptation is pretty much constant! Some women practically throw themselves at me! It's crazy! And one time after a huge fight with my wife, I lost the battle with temptation which I have regretted ever since. It is not any excuse or looking for some understanding, I am just trying to explain why my wife and I are separated." explained Ashley sadly.

"I am very sorry to hear about the hardship in your marriage," Molly said sincerely.

"It is fine. It was me who ruined my wife's trust and it is me who needs to rebuild it. Thank you very much, Molly."

"For what?" asked Molly.

"For listening! For not judging! Your opinion matters to me a lot and I wanted you to know that I am not one of those superficial people."

"The saying comes to mind: 'Do not judge a book by its cover!'" said Molly with a big smile.

They both finished their lunch and Ashley paid the bill with the company's card, as promised. Then, they headed out to the next meeting …

8

It was Friday night and Molly and Sam decided together that it would be best if Mark joined them during their drinks with others from the office.

They all decided that it would be the easiest way for Mark to finally meet Molly.

Earlier that day it was a very busy Friday in the office. Despite that Molly managed to speak to Ashley. He was very excited because he was spending the whole weekend with his family, even his wife. He admitted to Molly that it seemed that things with his marriage were going in the right direction. This is why he decided to miss the office drinks in order to get rest before a very important weekend.

Even Emily was surprisingly nice to Molly that day. Molly decided to enjoy it while it lasted and not to question Emily's reasons for being nice towards her.

Sam was very busy too but he could not hide his excitement that Molly and Mark would finally meet that evening. He even came over to Molly's desk and said,

"Molly, I know you are very busy but I cannot wait for you to meet my Mark. Sorry, but I had to tell you that just now!"

"I am very excited too!" replied Molly.

They both went back then to their respective jobs.

After lunch, the hours went fast and it turned out to be evening very soon, at least for Molly. She managed to finish all she had planned for herself for that afternoon and joined the others for drinks.

Maybe half an hour tops since they had all started, Sam came over to Molly, who was standing in a queue at the bar, and said that Mark was there. She followed Sam in order to meet Mark. Suddenly they stopped and Sam called out, "Mark, I would like you to finally meet my friend Molly!"

The guy who was standing with his back towards them turned around and Molly could not believe her eyes. Standing in the front of her was the mystery guy from the tube.

"It is you!" Molly said, very surprised.

"I should say the same!" said a very surprised Mark.

"Do you know each other?" asked a confused Sam.

"Well …no!" said Molly. "Small world, isn't it?"

"No …we do not know each other by name! Small world indeed!" said Mark with a big smile on his face.

"Sam, do you remember about this mystery guy from the tube? This is him!" said Molly enthusiastically.

"Sam, do you recall me talking about the girl in the tube squeezing my knee when it got pitch black suddenly? This is her!" said Mark enthusiastically.

"Yes …I can remember both of you telling me your stories from the tube! Ha ha …small world indeed!" Sam said with less confusion now. "Molly this is Mark and Mark please meet Molly!"

"Very nice to finally meet you Molly! It is very nice to put a face to person, who is such a very good friend to my Sam. Thank you again for your patience, understanding and good advice on the importance of open communication in our relationship," said Mark with extreme gratitude.

"Pleasure is mine, Mark! Always happy to help if I can be of any use!"

The three of them spent some time together, trying to get to know each other better, especially Molly and Mark, as they both knew how important it was to Sam that they eventually know each other and enjoy each other's company. They had all had a few drinks each and shared lots of stories with one another, when Mark announced that he needed to leave. He'd promised his younger sister to escort her to their parents' home. Sam quickly realized that he'd completely forgot about it.

"It was very nice to finally meet you, Molly. Have a fun night guys with your mates from your work. See you at home Sam! Till later Molly!" said Mark.

"Great to meet you, Mark!" Molly replied.

"See you soon, Mark!" Sam replied.

Mark left and Molly and Sam joined their work colleagues for more drinks until the closing of the bar. The majority decided to call it a night, as did Molly and Sam. However, they both decided to hunt for a shop selling water on their way home, as they were both extremely thirsty. They said their goodbyes to their office mates and began their hunt.

They were walking through one of the roundabouts on Oxford Street and talking about Mark being Molly's mystery guy from the tube and how it was good that she hadn't invested herself in him, as it would be a lost cause anyway.

Suddenly, a voice from a group of people, said,

"Hi Molly!"

Molly turned her head in direction of the voice and replied, "OMG …hi Luke …what are you doing here at this time?"

Molly was also trying to hide the fact that she was blushing after seeing Luke.

"Well …it is Simon's, one of my best friends, it's his birthday today and we are celebrating!" Luke responded and moved towards Molly, leaving the rest behind. Approaching Molly and Sam he asked, "And what are you doing here, Molly?"

"Well …we have had an office drinks tonight …Luke, I would like to introduce my friend Sam, we work together," said Molly, trying even harder to hide the fact she was blushing even more.

"Very nice to meet you, Sam," said Luke.

"Very nice to meet you, Luke," replied Sam.

"I'd better go back to my friends!" said Luke suddenly. "It was nice to meet you Sam and it was great to see you Molly! Take care guys!"

"It was nice to meet you too. Bye," said Sam.

"See you soon Luke!" Molly responded, still blushing a little.

Luke turned around to go back to his friends. When he was approaching them, he heard the question suddenly:

"Who are they?" asked Simon curiously.

"Well, that is Molly and her friend from work, Sam."

"That's Molly? The one you have a crush on?" asked Simon

"Yeah!"

"Man …I would say that she is out of your league! … But at the same time, you should at least try. They say that it is better to regret what you have done than regretting that you have done nothing!" said Simon.

"You are right, Simon! But for now, we should go back to celebrating your birthday" replied little bit embarrassed Luke.

Sam waited until Luke was further away and could not hear them before asking Molly: "Who was that?"

"That was my neighbour / landlord, Luke." responded Molly.

"That's Luke?" you could hear the surprise in Sam's voice.

"Hmm …yes!" confirmed Molly.

"No wonder that you are blushing so much!"

"Oh …no! Do you think that he has seen it too?" asked worried Molly.

"No! Besides, I do not think that he knows you as well as I do!"

"That is great!" said Molly with huge relief in her voice. and continued "What an eventful evening! I have finally met your Mark and you have managed to put a face to all the stories about my neighbour that you had heard a lot about before!"

"What a face!" said Sam and momentarily started to laugh and Molly joined him.

After maybe ten minutes after meeting Luke, they both decided that it was high time to finish their hunt for water and get back home. They took a taxi …

9

At first Molly's family were very much against her plans to start everything over and relocate to London by herself. They thought that it was a mad idea and that it was too late for that. Her parents especially were disapproving of these plans. They could not understand why she would give up her seemingly perfect life and want to start from the beginning. They also were convinced that Nathan was a perfect guy for their daughter, not knowing the dooming reality. Nathan loved himself, his job and then Molly, in that order. Molly was eventually honest with her parents regarding the relationship with Nathan and they understood at last that her decision was very difficult but necessary.

Once Molly moved to London and it seemed that she was happier, her parents changed their minds and were more supportive. They both even visited her on a few occasions and were in fact very happy that she had made that crazy decision to start over in London.

Her only sibling, her older brother Matthew, was more supportive of her decision to relocate to London from the outset. This was because he knew more about the real relationship between his sister and her boyfriend much earlier than their parents did. Molly and Matthew were quite close and this did not change when she moved out from their hometown. That is why it was not alarming when Matthew sent Molly a text message to ask if he could visit her that coming weekend. Besides, he'd already been for a few weekends in London to visit her.

The weekend came and Matthew visited as was planned, however his visit was not as energizing as Molly had expected. At the beginning, the siblings' meeting was very enjoyable for both but the tone had changed when Molly asked about Pamela.

"So how is Pamela?"

"Well …I do not know!" Matthew responded.

"What do you mean by saying that you do not know?" asked confused Molly.

"Well …I do not know because we are not together anymore!"

"What?" said a surprised Molly, her mouth wide opened. After a few minutes she continued with the line of questioning: "What again? Why? When?"

"You were aware that we were having some problems?" asked Matthew, a bit confused.

"Yes …But I would not ever have expected that you were not together in a million years! How long has it been?

"Well …almost eight years …and would be longer if not the fact it became a little too crowded for me as it turned out Pamela had found herself another man!" said Matthew with real disappointment and anger in his voice and maybe after a minute or two he continued: "I was right in thinking that something was odd between us! You remember when I told you during our last conversations that I felt that something had been wrong between Pamela and I for some time …how stupid of me thinking then that it could have been related to the fact that I am eight years older than she is! You know …different attitudes to life!"

"Matthew, I do not know what to say!" said a very sad and totally shocked Molly and she added after few moments: "When did you break up?"

"It is quite fresh …It happened on the day I texted you regarding my visit. After Pamela and I broke up, I decided on the spot that I needed to change my settings and I needed to do it right away or very soon and that is why I texted you." explained Matthew

"So, this has happened this week?"

"Yeah!" confirmed Matthew.

"Matthew, I really do not know what to say. At least you know now and not when you were married! I have never been in a similar situation so I know it is easier for me to say! I have never been in a relationship with such a substantial age gap."

"The age difference did not help. On the contrary, it turned out that we both wanted something different. Why could not she just be open and honest with me instead of cheating on me?"

"Maybe she was not as perfect as you imagined and believed her to be! You had that perfect picture of Pamela in your head and no one or nothing could ever change it!"

"Maybe … "

"Do not worry, Matthew! Everything will be fine and I am sure of that! You are a strong and resilient guy and it does not look just now like that but with time you will find your own happiness! It is never too late!" Molly said with confidence.

"Thanks, Sis! I really appreciate that you have allowed me to visit you this weekend and that you have listened to me," said Matthew with huge appreciation.

"Not a problem at all, Matthew!"

"Ok …it is high time to stop moaning about things! Let us talk about something else!

"Sure! Do you remember your obsession with football, when we were kids?"

"Well, to be perfectly honest, it still is my obsession, just in another way because I am older!"

"That is ok. I just hope that you are not so bossy as you were with me! I still remember running after the ball on the hot sand at the beach! I was the goalkeeper and obviously always had to bring the ball back, when you kicked it somewhere far away!"

"Ha ha, I do remember that! We were kids and our problems were smaller," said Matthew nostalgically.

"I also still remember that you made me give you random scores in order for you to decide the winner of your imaginative football league! I will never forget about your little football notebook, where you were collecting all those scores." Molly tried to lighten the mood.

"Do you really remember that?" asked a surprised Matthew.

"Yes, I do! I remember many crazy things that we were doing as small kids but we will reminisce some other time! I am very hungry, and you?"

"Actually …yes I am."

"That is great. I would like to treat you to a lunch in the nearby café."

"Thanks, Sis!"

They both went to the café and had some very tasty food. After eating they went back to Molly's flat in order to rest before they headed into the centre for a few drinks.

Before they left the flat, Matthew could not resist his favourite banana milkshake, of which Molly had bought a few specially for his visit.

10

It was already after ten on Sunday morning when Molly and Matthew decided to go out for breakfast. They went back to the same place that they had had their meal the day before. It was Molly who decided to treat her brother again.

After the delicious breakfast they were on the way to Molly's flat, when they met Luke.

"Hi Molly!" said Luke enthusiastically.

"Hi Luke!" Molly responded with huge enthusiasm too.

"OMG …no Way! It is really you?" asked Luke with consternation.

"Wow! It is you! I cannot believe my eyes!" said a surprised Matthew.

"Hi Matt …It has been ages!" responded Luke.

"Yeah …Long time no see Luke!" said Matthew.

"How do you know each other?" asked a confused Molly.

"Well …we used to study together!" responded Luke with a big smile.

"Yeah! That was a great time!" confirmed Matthew with a big smile too.

"Matt, how do you know Molly?" asked Luke.

"She is my younger sister, Luke, how do you know my sister?"

"Believe it or not, we are neighbours, aren't we Molly?" Luke responded, looking at Molly.

"So, you are this Luke …" started Matthew but remembered suddenly the conversation with his sister and stopped and asked a few moments later, "Luke, would you like to catch up later?"

"That would be great! I am in fact in a bit of hurry just now" explained Luke.

"Great! Let's say in three hours, around half past three?"

"Sure! I will be back by then. Pop round to mine." said Luke.

"I would prefer it if you popped in to Molly's," said Matthew swiftly and he added, "Sis, is it ok for Luke and I to catch up at yours later?"

"Sure!" replied Molly and she thought to herself, *That is actually perfect!*

"Ok …that is set then …Luke, you are coming to Molly's at half past three!"

"Sure!" replied Luke.

"See you soon!" said Matthew.

"See you soon, guys!" responded Luke enthusiastically.

"Till later Luke!" responded Molly. She was blushing a little bit and thought to herself, *Thank God neither Matthew or Luke noticed that I was blushing a bit ……uff…!*

Luke went one way, whereas Molly and Matthew went in the opposite direction. It took them ten minutes to get to Molly's flat. Matthew offered his sister a warm drink as he started to make one for himself soon after they entered the flat. Molly was still very full after the breakfast and therefore she did not take Matthew up on his offer.

"So Sis, tell me, is my friend Luke, that Luke? That dreamy neighbour /new landlord from our conversations?"

"And what do you think?" responded a blushing Molly.

"I think it is him! It must be him!"

"Hm …why must be?" asked Molly.

"Well …he is a really nice guy and you are simply great! I think you would make a very nice couple!"

"So, you are not mad, that your younger sister likes your friend?"

"Not at all! On the contrary!"

"That is very good, because I do really like him!" said Molly with pure honesty in her voice.

"I think that he likes you too!" Matthew teased Molly.

"That is great but please, Matthew! Promise me …that you won't mention to Luke anything about our conversation!" said a worried Molly.

"Ok!" Matthew agreed.

"Ok …I do like him but I would like things to go their natural way …it means no involvement on your part! Do you promise, Matthew?" asked Molly seriously.

"I do promise, Sis!" Matthew said, convincing Molly with the tone of his voice.

Molly and Matthew finished their conversation regarding Luke way before he was supposed to come to visit them. After the conversation regarding Molly's love life, the siblings started to exchange their experiences of the first day in the new job, swiftly moving to their parents and different stories from their childhood.

Molly and Matthew had a lot of fun reminiscing about their childhood but Luke came on time and the conversation shifted to times during Matthew and Luke's studies. Molly was blushing again and therefore she decided to hide herself in her bedroom for a little while under false pretenses of giving the guys time to catch up. She went to her bedroom, closed the door and said quietly to herself, *Get a grip Molly! Stop blushing! It will be you who ruins everything, not Matthew!*

It took her a little while to stop blushing. She came back to the living room and when she did, Matthew and Luke continued their conversation. Matthew said that it was very unfortunate that he and Luke hadn't met earlier, when he had been visiting Molly before. He also happily answered Luke's question regarding the fact that Molly was calling him by his full name. He explained that they'd always been called by their full names by their parents and it had stuck and therefore both Molly and himself used each other's full names.

Luke's visit was very short, therefore the guys decided to have a proper catch up very soon with Matthew coming to London again or Luke visiting his hometown. They had also exchanged their current phone numbers, which turned out to be the same as during their studies a good few years ago.

Once Luke left it was time for Matthew to pack himself up and leave Molly's flat and to take a taxi to the train station. Before he left, Molly saved Luke's phone number in her mobile, trying to convince Matthew and herself that it was just in case.

Matthew thanked his sister for having him for the past two days and treating him to different meals and drinks, for listening to his moans about Pamela and for trying to lift his spirits and giving him important advice. He also said that he hoped that the thing with Luke would happen soon and that Molly must keep him informed about this situation.

11

It was already Thursday. Molly had a feeling that it would be an interesting day, full of surprises and her intuition did not let her down.

Molly came to the office early as usual. Sam, Ashley and a few other people were there too. They all expected another busy day ahead like Molly did and decided to try to beat the time and to start their job early.

Molly started to work straight away and was very surprised when Sam came over to her desk and said it was lunchtime. They went to a nearby place serving lunch and Sam offered to pay the bill. Molly was trying to change his mind but he insisted and she eventually agreed. At first, she was a little confused but over the course of the lunch she understood the reason why Sam was insisting on paying.

"Molly, there is something important I need to tell you!" said Sam very seriously.

"Are you sick? Someone has died? You have broken up with Mark?" asked a worried Molly.

"No, nothing like that! Calm down!" said Sam reassuringly and he continued "It is to do with you!"

"Oh …come on Sam …just say it like it is …I really do not know what are you trying to say" replied Molly. You could hear the frustration in her voice.

"I regret to ruin your day!"

"What?"

"Well …I cannot go with you to your friend's wedding as some family matter has suddenly appeared and I will have to go back home that weekend," said Sam apologetically.

"But the wedding is in ten days! What will I do?" asked sadly Molly.

"I know that it is very soon and I have promised that I would be there with you. I am so very sorry but there is nothing I could do about my family emergency," Sam responded with all the seriousness and concern in his voice.

"I totally understand that a family matter is an issue which is way more important than some wedding," said Molly calmly, you could hear the concern in her voice too.

"If I told you that there was a solution to your problem, would you be interested in hearing it?"

"Sure!" Molly responded enthusiastically.

"Well …you want me there for the support, right?"

"Right!"

"You want to make your ex Nathan jealous and to show him that you have moved on, right?"

"Yeah! Where are you going with this, Sam?"

"Wait a minute …I will explain! If I told you that you still could have all of that but it would be Mark instead of me, who would go with you to that wedding? I have already spoken to him and he is more than happy to do that and pretend to be your new boyfriend! What do you think about that, Molly?" asked Sam with little bit of hope in his voice.

"Well …I think that it is a very crazy idea! But also a good one …taking into account that time is of the essence actually! Are you totally sure that Mark would be up for it?"

"Yes, I am sure of this as it was his idea in fact! He suggested it himself after we learned about my family emergency last night. He said actually that it would be great to spend more time with you!"

"That is great! You will not be there but I will not be alone when facing Nathan!" said Molly with a note of optimism in her voice.

"Exactly! Molly, I am really sorry for causing you a problem."

"It is ok! It happens! You maybe have caused me a problem but you also have found a solution! I am very sorry about your family emergency. We can talk about it whenever you are ready," responded Molly with concern in her voice.

"Thanks for everything, Molly. Thanks for understanding! You are the best!"

"No problem, Sam!"

Molly and Sam finished their lunch and Sam dealt with the bill as he had insisted on before. It was high time to leave the place that they dined in and get back to the office. On their way back, Sam explained to Molly that it was very late at night when he and Mark had got to know about his family emergency and that is why he did not mention it earlier to her as they both, Molly and him, had to have a good chat about the wedding first. He also added that he would like to talk to her about his family emergency but he wanted to deal with it first.

They got back to the office and Molly hoped that she could get on with her work. She had already sat down in the chair at her desk, when she saw the message on her computer from Ashley, asking her to pop in to his office, whenever she had a moment to spare. She decided not to postpone it and went to Ashley's office right away.

"Oh …it is you Molly!" said Ashley with surprise in his voice and added "I was not expecting you to pop in so soon!"

"Hi Ashley! Should I come back later?" asked Molly.

"No! No! I just assumed that you would pop in later but now is actually fine!"

"That is great! How can I help then?" Molly asked with a big smile.

"Well …to be perfectly honest …this matter is not even related to our work!" Ashley said with a little guilt in his voice and added, "I just wanted to share some good news with you!"

The phone rang once and then it continued to ring.

"I have to take this! Excuse me just for a minute," Ashley said decisively.

"Sure!" replied Molly quickly.

Ashley quickly answered the phone and Molly could hear only what he was saying.

"Yes, speaking …Oh no! …Really? …You are joking, right? …But the party is this weekend! …

Yes, in two days! …What should we do now? …You are very sorry, really? This is not the end of that, I am pretty sure! …Good day to you Sir too!" He put the phone down.

Ashley was very angry about the whole conversation he'd had about the music at Saturday's party.

"Are you ok? Is everything all right?" asked a concerned Molly.

"Well …no! You are aware of the department party we are having this weekend?"

"Obviously!"

"Guy has just called to say that they would not make it! The band will not make it as the most of its members are really under the weather and not able to play and sing!"

"OMG! But the party is on this Saturday, in just two days?" said Molly with huge concern in her voice.

"Exactly!" Ashley raised his voice. "What will I do now? No one will be now free in two days! This is a huge disappointment and a real disaster!"

"Calm down Ashley! There might be a solution to your problem. Not something that you had in mind but time is of the essence!" said Molly confidently.

"What do you have there, Molly?"

"Well …nothing yet for certain! My neighbour/current landlord Luke is a DJ. Not professionally, I don't think. Long story short, I have seen DJ's decks in his flat on a few occasions! I have his number. I could contact him and try to convince him to play for us on Saturday!"

"I bet you could!" said Ashley with a cheeky smile and continued: "You are right that I did not have a DJ in mind but I am very desperate just now so it will have to do, if he agrees! Fingers crossed!"

Molly advised Ashley that she would let him know straight away when she heard from Luke and she got back to her desk to contact him.

12

Molly got back to her desk and texted Luke. *Hi Luke! It is Molly – your neighbour here. I am very sorry to disturb you but I have a bit of an emergency and I need to speak to you urgently! Please call me when you have an opportunity to talk! Hopefully sooner than later! Thanks, Molly.*

She put her phone down on her desk and started to work. Molly was keeping her mobile phone on the desk, which was normally not allowed, but authorised in this instance by Ashley in case Luke contacted her back.

Luke checked his phone and noticed that he had a text message from Molly. He read it thoroughly and panicked a bit. He decided to call her straight away.

Suddenly, her mobile phone started to vibrate. It was Luke and she picked up.

"Hello!" said Molly.

"Hello Molly! It is Luke here. Are you ok? I have just got your text message concerning some emergency!" said a worried Luke.

"I am fine! Really! The emergency concerns my work actually! First things first, do you have any plans for Saturday?" Molly asked.

"This Saturday? No! Why?" asked a curious Luke.

"Well …we have the department party on this Saturday and the band has just pulled out. Ashley, my boss, has been very sad and stressed about it and I may have mentioned to him that I had seen your DJ decks! Are you mad at me?"

"First of all, I am not mad at you! But Molly, I am not a professional DJ! I have never played in front of people!"

"I know and I would never ask you about it if it was not an emergency!"

"I know! But …do they even know that I am not a professional? I would not like to cause any problems for you!" said Luke with a hint of worry in his voice.

"Ashley knows that and he is desperate. Besides, you would not cause any problems, on the contrary, you would resolve our issue. After all, even an amateur DJ is better than music from a computer!" said Molly, trying to convince Luke.

"I suppose …" Luke replied and added after a moment, "Ok, I will do it!"

"Really?"

"Yes, really!"

"Thank you very much! Luke you are the best. I owe you big time!" said Molly with relief.

"We will see if you think the same after this weekend!" said Luke with a little concern in his voice and added: "I am very sorry but I have to go now. See you later, Molly!"

"No problem! Once again thank you very much! I will pop in to yours later with some details. See you later Luke!" responded Molly with a big smile on her face.

"Bye!"

"Bye!" said Molly.

Both Molly and Luke hung up in order to get back to their tasks.

As promised, Molly went to Ashley's office in order to pass on the good news. She barged into there with a big smile.

"Hi again Ashley!" said Molly enthusiastically.

"Hi Molly," responded Ashley.

"Success! My neighbour Luke agreed to play at our department party this weekend!"

"OMG Molly that is great! You are a star! Thank you very much for your help! You cannot even imagine how much it means to me! Thanks a lot!" said a relieved Ashley.

"I am not the one to thank! Now, the problem with music at the party is sorted, what did you want to chat to me about in the first place?"

"Oh yeah, that! I just wanted to share some news with you. I spent the whole weekend with my family. Baby steps with my wife, it is all going slowly but surely!"

"I am so happy for you!" replied Molly.

"In fact, we are having another weekend together again!" said Ashley enthusiastically.

"Weekend? But we are having this department party?" asked Molly curiously.

"Not this weekend but the next one."

"Wow! I am going to my friend's wedding that weekend!" said Molly with a huge smile. "Anyway, I'd better get back to my desk! After all the job will not do itself …bye Ashley!"

"Bye Molly! Thank you very much again!" said Ashley.

Molly got back to her desk and got stressed a bit because she had a lot to do that afternoon. She was so busy that she did not notice how much time had passed. It was already after the time she had been supposed to finish. The office was a bit deserted when she actually finished and decided to go home.

On the way back home, she remembered that she had promised Luke to visit him that evening in order to give him more details regarding Saturday's party. She decided to go home first, have some food and refresh herself, as she did not want to visit Luke looking untidy and tired. She would not admit it even to herself but his opinion really mattered to her.

Luke admitted to Molly that he had been stressing about Saturday ever since he had agreed to play. In order to calm him down, she suggested that the pair of them prepare the list of essential songs for Luke to have on Saturday. Making the list took them much longer than expected but they both had a lot of fun and therefore they did not mind that a lot of time passed. They were really enjoying each other's company.

Saturday had come and it stressed Luke again, although Molly confirmed again that her boss knew that being a DJ was just hobby for him. He was very nervous at first, especially after arriving at Molly's office. However, with time and the good reception of his musical mixing, he started to loosen up and enjoy himself. Maybe seeing the person he knew or the fact that he really had a crush on her, or simply a bit of both, Luke seemed to be more relaxed when Molly eventually showed up.

The party was a success. Despite the fact that Molly's co-workers knew that Luke was not a professional DJ, they advised him that he should think about it professionally. This really came as a big surprise to him and boosted his confidence a bit. Molly was full of praise for him too. She thanked him for saving the party. She also enthusiastically said again that he was a star and that she owed him big time. Luke just smiled adorably and decided not to say anything, because he did not want to sound too strange and rude again.

On Monday morning, when Molly came to the office, Ashley asked her to his office again.

"Hi Ashley!" said Molly, walking in to his office and added, "You wanted to see me? How can I help?"

"Hi Molly! I just wanted to say that the party on Saturday was a big success! And all thanks to you! I really appreciate you!"

"But I did nothing!" said Molly quietly.

"Not true Molly! You managed to somehow convince your neighbour in less than an hour to be a DJ at our department party. This was brilliant, Molly! I always had high regard for you but your eagerness to help and being full of ideas surprised even me! Thank you again!" said Ashley proudly.

"Thank you very much for your kind words, Ashley!" replied Molly, a little embarrassed and she got back eventually to her desk.

13

It was a sunny Saturday. Molly had just woken up and remembered that it was the day when she would see Nathan again. It was quite a scary perspective but she also remembered that she had Mark with her, ready to pretend to be her boyfriend in order to be her support and make Nathan feel jealous.

Molly decided to make herself look pretty. She'd bought herself a new dress and shoes especially for the occasion. She could wear one of her many dresses she already owned but she wanted this teal one to impress others, especially Nathan. All came together, even make-up and hair, she simply looked beautiful.

The time came and Mark showed up as previously agreed. When he saw Molly, he could not believe his eyes.

"Molly, you simply look stunning, you …I mean that you just look breathtaking!" said Mark, staring at her.

"Thank you very much for your kind words, Mark!" replied Molly, a bit embarrassed.

"For sure, Nathan will be really jealous!" added Mark after a few moments.

"We need to go now or we will be late. I really hate being late!" said Molly, just after looking at the clock hanging in the hall. "Mark, are you ready to pretend to be my boyfriend for few hours? By the way, you don't look so shabby yourself!"

"Thank you very much Molly! And yes, I am very ready!"

Both of them, Molly and Mark, left Molly's flat and took a taxi to the wedding. One of her friends from her studies – the bride herself – had invited her to this wedding. Nathan was the groom's guest, so it meant that no matter what had happened between him and Molly, he would always be invited to this wedding.

The ceremony started on time. Later, all the wedding guests were taken into a huge wedding venue and the party really started. Molly and Mark were also in this venue, when Molly noticed Nathan. She knew that she had to be strong and act naturally, especially with Mark, in order to make Nathan feel jealous. Her heart was pounding so she grabbed Mark's hand even tighter. Nathan also noticed Molly and moved in her direction.

"Hi Molly!" said Nathan, kissing both her cheeks.

"Hi Nathan!" responded Molly politely.

"Must say that you look just amazing!" said Nathan.

He'd always been so confident that he did not even notice that Molly and Mark were holding hands. He would never have expected that Molly could already have a boyfriend. Molly had surprised him though.

"Thank you very much for your kind words Nathan! Let me introduce my boyfriend Mark," said Molly enthusiastically.

"Excuse me?" said a confused and shocked Nathan.

"Let me introduce my boyfriend, Mark," repeated Molly patiently.

"Nice to meet you, Mark! I am Nathan, the ex!" said a still shocked Nathan.

"Nice to meet you! Molly has never mentioned her ex by name!" said Mark cheekily.

Molly was simply very grateful for his acting skills.

"Oh really?" asked a surprised Nathan.

"Yes, really!" responded Mark confidently.

"I am sorry but I need to speak with the groom. It was nice to meet you, Mark. And it was nice to see you Molly. Catch you later guys!" said Nathan after a minute and then he left.

He looked little bit confused and surprised that Molly had a boyfriend already. His confidence in himself has been weakened a bit. Molly could not believe her eyes when he looked genuinely shocked having learned about Mark. She was very happy about it and therefore she wanted to express her gratitude to Mark.

"OMG! That was amazing Mark! I have never seen Nathan so worried and surprised when you said that I had never mentioned his name! Genius!" said an excited and grateful Molly.

"I could not stop myself! Stupid! Hopefully, he will learn a lesson!" responded Mark.

"What lesson?" asked Molly curiously.

"That he made a huge mistake letting you leave"

"Thank you Mark for your kindness!"

"I really mean it! He has behaved very stupidly. Mister Confidence loving himself the most!" said Mark and still holding Molly's hand, he pulled her delicately and they went to the seating area.

They were not sitting close to Nathan and it was much better, as both Molly and Mark seemed more relaxed than in his presence. Lots of fun and laughter, eating and drinking and lots of dancing indicated that they both were having a great time at this wedding. Molly felt that Nathan was watching her, especially when she was dancing with Mark but he never came by to talk to them again, as mentioned previously.

Molly was very surprised that she was actually enjoying herself while being a guest at the same wedding as her ex.

"Thank you very much Mark for pretending so well to be my boyfriend and for making Nathan feel jealous! I really appreciate it!" said Molly suddenly.

"It is my pleasure! I was not expecting to have so much fun with it!" responded Mark enthusiastically.

Mark and Molly were in fact very good in pretending to be a couple, as other guests, including Nathan, were sure of that, because of their way of dancing together and the attentiveness and intimacy between them both.

This time Molly decided to take some cosmetics with her to the bathroom in order to refresh herself and her make-up a little bit. It was in fact a good idea, as the rest of the guests started to join for the evening celebrations.

Molly and Mark were sitting at the table and talking when suddenly Molly got up and went in the direction of the crowd of evening guests. She could not believe her eyes.

"Hi Luke!" said Molly enthusiastically.

"Wow! Hi Molly!" responded a confused Luke.

"Small world!" said a positively surprised Molly.

"Yeah! Very small!" answered Luke.

"What are you doing here?"

"Well …I could ask you the same question! Well …my granny Jenny is actually a very close friend of the groom's family. Due to her recent and unplanned visit to Australia, I was nominated by her to represent her at this wedding! And why are you here?"

"Well, we are here because I am friends with the bride."

"Must say that you look breathtaking Molly!"

"Thank you very much Luke!" said a flustered Molly and she added after a few moments, "Better get back to the table. I have left Mark alone with a bunch of strangers!"

"Sure! I will not keep you any longer."

That Saturday morning Luke had decided to listen to Simon's advice and tell Molly about his feelings for her soon but his biggest nightmare came to life – Molly had a boyfriend, at least that was what he thought.

Because of that Luke did not have a good time and decided to go home after a few hours, despite the fact that he'd promised Jenny to be there instead of her. Meanwhile, Molly had a very good time with Mark and enjoyed herself a lot.

14

Molly has had a very good time with Mark at the recent wedding but it was high time to get back to reality for them both. She and Mark had just been pretending to be a couple in order to fool Nathan especially and she came to the realization that she was actually single.

On Monday evening Sam sent her a text message reminding her about Thursday's blind date that she'd agreed to go on. Actually Mark had organised it some time ago, as a way of thanking Molly again for listening and advising Sam on his troubles with his relationship with Mark.

Thursday came very fast for Molly, as *promise is a promise* she thought to herself. Her working day passed very fast too, as usual. Her date was in a small bar in the heart of London. She refreshed herself and her make-up after finishing work and left the office for this bar. The stroll took her around ten minutes and she was there by six, as agreed. She could not believe her eyes, as the first person she saw there was Luke. She decided to go up to him after all.

"Hi Luke!" said a confused Molly.

"Hi Molly!" replied an also confused Luke.

"Small world! We keep bumping to each other!" said Molly with a big smile.

"Yes …small world indeed!" replied Luke.

"What are you doing here?" asked Molly

"Well …I could ask you the same thing! I am here for a blind date!"

"Me too! Do you think that it is possible that we both have a blind date with each other?" asked inquisitively Molly.

Luke's heart started to beat faster and he thought to himself that it was like Christmas again when he heard her asking the last question but he tried his best not to show exaltation.

"I was told to be here at six. My friend told me that his friend Mark was trying to set up this nice girl with some guy and my friend thought about me."

"Yeah …the name of the guy who organised that for me is Mark too! You have seen my Mark too."

"Where?"

"At the wedding with me last weekend!" explained Molly.

"I thought that it was your boyfriend!"

"Who, Mark? No, he is just my friend! We were just pretending that we were a couple in order to fool my ex and make him jealous! Actually, Mark is a boyfriend of my friend Sam, who was originally to accompany me at this wedding but he was not able to in the end and that is why Mark decided to step in and he was my first pretend date!"

"I must say that you fooled me as well! I really thought that he was your boyfriend! Which made me very sad." admitted Luke.

"No, no …I am single …I would not be here if I was not!" said Molly firmly. "I could not do it to someone because I would not want them to do it to me!"

"Totally understand and agree with you, Molly!"

"Do you remember my friend Sam?" asked Molly suddenly.

"No, I do not think so! Should I?"

"Well …he is the guy that I introduced you to at my work party night when you were celebrating your friend's birthday that evening. We all met near Oxford Circus actually."

"Oh …yeah! I do remember Sam!"

"That is great! So, Mark, who was with me at that wedding, and Sam are actually together! And it was Mark who organised this blind date! He must have asked his friend, who is also your friend, for help in finding a date for me!"

“Mystery solved! Good on you, Sherlock!” said Luke with a big smile

“Well …thank you Doctor Watson!” responded Molly, laughing. She continued with a more serious tone. “It must be him who organised this, from what you have told me and from what I know myself.”

“I would say that it does not matter anymore! I am very happy how it’s worked out in the end and I would prefer to focus on getting to know you better, if you are still up for it, Molly?!” said firmly Luke.

“I am very sorry! I did not mean to be so geeky or rude!” said an embarrassed Molly. “Truth be told, I am quite nervous and I was trying to hide it by talking about Mark and Sam.”

“Oh …I see! Do not worry! I am nervous too!” said a relieved Luke. “Let us get to know each other …I will start first then.”

They broke the ice with chat about the wedding they had both been to and about Luke recently receiving lots of praise from Molly’s work colleagues for his DJ skills. Then, Luke started to talk about himself, his family and hometown. His stories about life helped Molly to relax a bit and share things about herself. She told Luke about the reasons behind moving to London not that long ago. She also explained why she needed Mark with her at the recent wedding.

They both enjoyed each other’s company so much that they did not notice that so much time had passed and the bar was shutting. Suddenly, Molly noticed the time and said to herself but loudly enough for Luke to hear, “OMG!”

“Is everything thing all right?” asked Luke, worried.

“Yes …it is totally fine! I have just noticed the time and I have a very busy schedule at work tomorrow! I need to go home like now. I am very sorry Luke!” said Molly and she grabbed her stuff and disappeared.

Luke was shocked a bit but checked the time himself and understood why Molly had left in such a hurry. He was not worried about their next meeting. He knew where he could find her after all.

Molly took a taxi and was home very quickly. She took a quick shower and went to bed but could not fall asleep for a long time. She kept thinking about Luke and his stories, about him only in a towel from the waist down, the time she interrupted his shower.

It was a sunny Friday morning when Molly's alarm went off and she woke up. She remembered last night with Luke and that put a huge smile on her face. She got ready for work and showed up in the office early, as usual. It was very much needed that day especially, taking into account her workload and very tight schedule. Nevertheless, although she was busy, she managed to speak to Sam about her blind date for a short period of time. He was positively surprised when he learned that this Luke was Molly's blind date. He knew exactly how much Molly fancied Luke, even before this date. He was actually very happy for Molly, that there was a ray of sunshine in her personal life too. Despite being very busy, Molly was in a very good mood all day. She had so much energy too, despite only a few hours of sleep. So much so, she decided to attend a yoga class in a local gym after her work. Being very sweaty, she decided to take a shower when someone started to knock at her door.

The blind date with Molly had put Luke in a very good mood too, so much so that he decided to tell her about it and invite her for the next date very soon.

"I am coming …Just a moment!" shouted Molly and she could not believe her eyes when she opened her door.

"Hi Molly, I hope that your day was not too busy!" said Luke with a big smile.

"It was crazy but I have managed, thanks for asking! I am very sorry for my look but I just came back home from the yoga class and was about to take a shower when you knocked!"

"No …I am very sorry for interrupting you. I did not mean to make you feel embarrassed and I just wanted you to know that I had a really good time yesterday."

"Me too!" said Molly enthusiastically.

"That is great!" replied Luke enthusiastically with a big smile. "That brings me to my question: would you like to grab a bite to eat with me very soon?"

"How soon?" asked Molly.

"Like tomorrow? But …If it is too soon, some other day! I just thought it is the weekend now so it would be easier for both of us," said Luke with a big smile and quite confidently.

"Yes, and yes …I would like that and tomorrow sounds good to me!" responded Molly enthusiastically.

"Great!" said Luke with relief in his voice. "How about lunch tomorrow then? I would like to pick you up around noon! Is that ok?"

"Lunch tomorrow at noon sounds good to me!" replied Molly with a bit of excitement in her voice.

"Great! See you tomorrow Molly!" said Luke and turned back to go to his flat.

"See you later Luke!" responded Molly while closing her door.

Molly closed the door, so no one could see her, and she did a little dance of happiness. It was not a prince on a white horse like in the books and cheesy rom-coms she simply adored, but she was not a princess either. She liked Luke and she knew now that the feeling was mutual and that was most important. She thought to herself, *Really it is never too late! How different my life was just few months ago!*

The End

www.ingramcontent.com/pod-product-compliance
Ingram Content Group UK Ltd.
Pitfield, Milton Keynes, MK11 3LW, UK
UKHW041957190726
13854UKWH00005B/2022